POWERED BY
The Oxford Picture Dictionary

WORKPLACE SKILLS BUILDER

OPD

Jayme Adelson-Goldstein

Norma Shapiro

Marjorie Fuchs

OXFORD
UNIVERSITY PRESS

OXFORD
UNIVERSITY PRESS

198 Madison Avenue
New York, NY 10016 USA

Great Clarendon Street, Oxford, OX2 6DP, United Kingdom

Oxford University Press is a department of the University of Oxford.
It furthers the University's objective of excellence in research, scholarship,
and education by publishing worldwide. Oxford is a registered trade
mark of Oxford University Press in the UK and in certain other countries

Director, ELT New York: Laura Pearson
Head of Adult, ELT New York: Stephanie Karras
Publisher, Academic English and Literacy: Sharon Sargent
Development Editor: Rebecca Meyer
Executive Art and Design Manager: Maj-Britt Hagsted
Design Project Manager: Michael Steinhofer
Image Manager: Trisha Masterson
Production Artists: Elissa Santos, Julie Sussman-Perez
Production Coordinator: Christopher Espejo

ISBN: 978 0 19 474075 3

Printed in China

This book is printed on paper from certified and well-managed sources

ACKNOWLEDGEMENTS

Illustrations by: Cover art, CUBE/Illustration Ltd; Tom White. Interior
illustration, Lori Anzalone; Gary Antonetti / Ortelius Design; Joe "Fearless"
Arenella/Will Sumpter; Argosy Publishing; Barbara Bastian; Ken Batelman;
Philip Batini/AA Reps; Thomas Bayley/Sparks Literary Agency; Sally Bensusen;
Eileen Bergman; Annie Bissett; Peter Bollinger/Shannon Associates; Higgens
Bond/Anita Grien; Molly Borman-Pullman; Kevin Brown; Andrea Champlin;
Mary Chandler; Jim Delapine; Jody Emery; Jim Fanning/Ravenhill Represents;
Mike Gardner; Garth Glazier/AA Reps; Von Glitschka/Scott Hull Associates;
Dennis Godfrey/Mike Wepplo; Steve Graham; Graphic Map & Chart Co.;
Julia Green/Mendola Art; Glenn Gustafson; Barbara Harmon; Ben Hasler/
NB Illustration; Betsy Hayes; Shelley Himmelstein; Matthew Holmes; Stewart
Holmes/Illustration Ltd.; Kev Hopgood; Janos Jantner / Beehive Illustration;
Pamela Johnson; Ken Joudrey/Munro Campagna; Bob Kaganich/Deborah
Wolfe; Steve Karp; Mike Kasun/Munro Campagna; Graham Kennedy; Uldis
Klavins / Hankins & Tegenborg, Ltd.; Marcel Laverdet/AA Reps; Jeffrey
Lindberg; Dennis Lyall/Artworks; Chris Lyons:/Lindgren & Smith; Scott
MacNeill; Alan Male/Artworks; Jeff Mangiat/Mendola Art; Mohammad Masoor;
Adrian Mateescu/The Studio; Karen Minot; Paul Mirocha/The Wiley Group;
Peter Miserendino/P.T. Pie Illustrations; Lee Montgomery/Illustration Ltd.;
Roger Motzkus; Laurie O'Keefe; Daniel O'Leary/Illustration Ltd.; Vilma
Ortiz-Dillon; Chris Pavely; Terry Pazcko; David Preiss/Munro Campagna;
Pronk & Associates; Tony Randazzo/AA Reps; Mark Reidy / Scott Hull
Associates; Mike Renwick/Creative Eye; Mark Riedy/Scott Hull Associates;
Jon Rogers/AA Reps; Zina Saunders; Jeff Sanson/Schumann & Co.; Stacey
Schuett; Rob Schuster; David Schweitzer/Munro Campagna; Ben Shannon/
Magnet Reps; Reed Sprunger/Jae Wagoner Artists Rep.; Studio Liddell/AA Reps;
Angelo Tillary; Anna Veltfort; Ralph Voltz/Deborah Wolfe; Jeff Wack/Mendola
Art; Brad Walker; Nina Wallace; Wendy Wassink; John White/The Neis Group;
Eric Wilkerson; Simon Williams/Illustration Ltd.; Lee Woodgate/Eye Candy
Illustration; Andy Zito; Craig Zuckerman.

*We would also like to thank the following for permission to reproduce the following
photographs*: istockphoto, pg. 21; kirstypargeter / istockphoto, pg. 26;
Alamy, pg. 26; Comstock / Age FotoStock, pg. 26; Rob Melnychuk / Jupiter
Images / Brand X, pg. 26; AbleStock / Jupiter Unlimited, pg. 26; MINORU KIDA /
Getty Images, pg. 26; ThinkStock / Age FotoStock, pg. 26; Dennis Kitchen /
OUP, pg. 26; Dennis Kitchen / OUP, pg. 48 – 49; Dennis Kitchen / OUP, pg. 54
and 56; Mlenny / istockphoto, pg. 60; Shutterstock, pg. 60; Keith Leighton /
Alamy, pg. 60; Shutterstock, pg 60; Ingram PublishingAge FotoStock, pg. 60;
Shutterstock, pg. 60; Urbano Delvalle/Time & Life Pictures/Getty Images,
pg. 60; Digitalvision/InMagine, pg. 60; gbrundin / istockphoto, pg. 60; Marek
Szumlas / shutterstock, pg. 78; Dennis Kitchen / OUP, pg. 78 – 79; Dennis
Kitchen / OUP, pg. 82; PunchStock, pg. 86; daizuoxin / shutterstock, pg. 86;
riekephotos / shutterstock, pg. 86; Marka / SuperStock, pg. 86; klikk /
istockphoto, pg. 86; SuperStock / SuperStock, pg. 86; Comstock / Jupiter
Unlimited, pg. 87; neen273 / istockphoto, pg. 87; istockphoto, pg. 87; dem10
/ istockphoto, pg. 87; Jupiter Images, pg. 87; Dennis Kitchen / OUP, pg. 90;
Digital Vision/Punch Stock, pg. 100; Photodisc / Age FotoStock, pg. 119;
Dennis Kitchen / OUP, pg. 127; REUTERS / Shannon Stapleton, pg. 132;
Dennis Kitchen / OUP, pg. 146 – 147; istockphoto, pg. 148: Comstock,
pg. 148; Dennis Kitchen / OUP, pg. 148; istockphoto, pg. 149; rsooll /
shutterstock, pg. 165; B.A.E. Inc. / Alamy, pg. 165; Brandon Laufenberg /
istockphoto, pg. 165; magicoven/shutterstock, pg. 165; mattesimages /
shutterstock, pg. 165; PhotoSpin, Inc / Alamy, pg. 165; Somos Images LLC /
Alamy, pg. 166.

WORKPLACE SKILLS BUILDER

Download Center

It's east to start!

Go to **www.oup.com/elt/opdworkplace**.

Downloadable video and audio allows students to study anytime, anywhere.

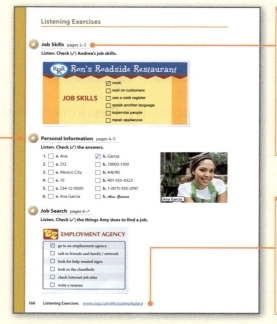

The Listening Practice section contains one listening exercise for every topic, reinforcing vocabulary while **building listening skills.**

Web address on the page makes it easy to find audio files, encouraging **independent practice** outside the classroom.

Online icon directs students to **download audio files.**

Practice activities allow students to use the words right away.

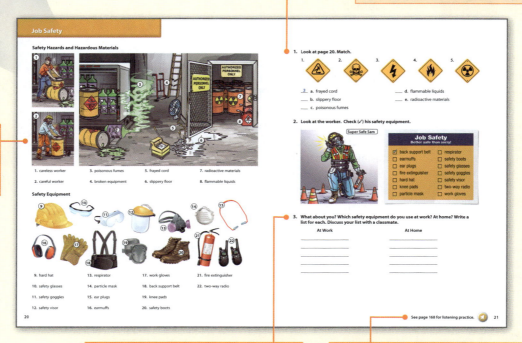

Visually clear and **richly contextualized illustrations** improve vocabulary acquisition.

Personalization exercises encourage students to **apply the vocabulary** to their work lives, making the new words relevant.

A reference on the page makes it easy to find the corresponding **listening exercise** at the back of the book.

Table of Contents

Contents

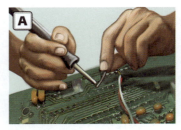
A. assemble components

B. assist medical patients

C. cook

D. do manual labor

E. drive a truck

F. fly a plane

G. make furniture

H. operate heavy machinery

I. program computers

J. repair appliances

K. sell cars

L. sew clothes

M. solve math problems

N. speak another language

O. supervise people

P. take care of children

Q. teach

R. type

S. use a cash register

T. wait on customers

Grammar Point: *can, can't*

*I am a chef. I **can** cook.*
*I'm not a pilot. I **can't** fly a plane.*
*I **can't** speak French, but I **can** speak Spanish.*

Role play. Talk to a job counselor.

A: *Tell me about your skills. Can you <u>type</u>?*
B: <u>*No, I can't*</u>, *but I <u>can use a cash register</u>.*
A: *OK. What other skills do you have?*

1. **Look at page 2. Circle the job skills in the job ads below. Then, write the name of the job. Use the words in the box.**

Administrative Assistant	Assembler	Carpenter	Chef	Childcare Worker
Home Health Care Aide	Manager	~~Salesperson~~	Server	Garment Worker

Job Title and Description	Company
a. ___*Salesperson*___ needed part-time to (sell cars) at our new Route 29 location. Must have experience and be able to work weekends.	Herb Rupert
b. _____ wanted to take care of small children. Part-time. Must speak English and Spanish. Experience and references required.	ChildCare
c. _____ wanted to assist medical patients. Good income. Experience required.	Medical Homecare
d. _____ needed to assemble telephone components in midtown factory. Immediate full-time employment.	Top Telecom
e. _____ wanted to make tables and chairs in our small shop.	Woodwork Corner
f. _____ wanted to supervise staff full-time at our small, friendly architecture company.	Nicolas Pyle, Inc.
g. _____ needed for busy law office. Must type 50 words per minute.	DeLucca, Smith, & Rotelli
h. _____ wanted to sew clothes in our downtown factory. Experience necessary.	L & H Clothing, Inc.
i. _____ wanted to cook everything from hamburgers to duck à l'orange at our small neighborhood restaurant.	The Corner Bistro
j. _____ needed to wait on customers at a busy downtown coffee shop. Part-time only. Experience preferred.	Kim's

2. **What about you? Check (✓) the job skills you have. Circle the skills you want to learn.**

- ☐ assemble components
- ☐ drive a truck
- ☐ operate heavy machinery
- ☐ sew clothes
- ☐ supervise people
- ☐ take care of children

- ☐ cook
- ☐ fly a plane
- ☐ program computers
- ☐ solve math problems
- ☐ teach
- ☐ Other: _____

- ☐ do manual labor
- ☐ make furniture
- ☐ repair appliances
- ☐ speak another language
- ☐ use a cash register
- ☐ Other: _____

See page 166 for listening practice.   3

A. Say your name.

B. Spell your name.

C. Print your name.

D. Sign your name.

Filling Out a Form

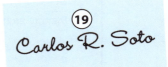

School Registration Form

1. name:

_____   _____   _____   _____

2. first name   3. middle initial   4. last name   5. address   6. apartment number

_____   _____   _____   (_____)   _____

7. city   8. state   9. ZIP code   10. area code   11. phone number

(_____)   _____ - _____   _____   _____

12. cell phone number   13. date of birth (DOB)   14. place of birth

_____ - ___ - _____   16. sex: 17. male ☐   _____

15. Social Security number   18. female ☐   19. signature

Pair practice. Make new conversations.

A: *My first name is Carlos.*
B: *Please spell Carlos for me.*
A: *C-a-r-l-o-s*

Ask your classmates. Share the answers.

1. Do you like your first name?
2. Is your last name from your mother? father? husband?
3. What is your middle name?

1. Look at page 4. What is Carlos Soto's . . . ?

a. ZIP code   <u>33607–3614</u>   c. apartment number   _____

b. area code   _____   d. Social Security number   _____

2. Match.

<u>9</u> a. middle initial   1. female

___ b. signature   2. California

___ c. city   3. (310)

___ d. sex   4. 548-00-0000

___ e. area code   5. Los Angeles

___ f. Social Security number   6. Miriam S. Shakter

___ g. name   7. 90049-1000

___ h. ZIP code   8. *Miriam S. Shakter*

___ i. state   9. S.

3. What about you? Fill out the form. Use your own information.

L.A. Adult Center

REGISTRATION FORM
(Please print.)

Last name _____   First name _____   Middle initial _____

Sex: ☐ Male   ☐ Female

Place of birth _____   Date of birth _____

Address _____   Apartment number _____

_____   _____
(City)   (State)   (ZIP code)

Phone _____   Cell phone _____

_____
Signature

See page 166 for listening practice.

A. **talk** to friends / **network**

B. **look in** the classifieds

C. **look for** help wanted signs

D. **check** Internet job sites

E. **go** to an employment agency

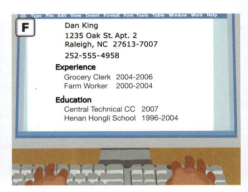

F. **write** a resume

G. **write** a cover letter

H. **send in** your resume and cover letter

I. **set up** an interview

J. **fill out** an application

K. **go on** an interview

L. **get** hired

1. **Look at page 6. Fill out Dan King's job application.**

EMPLOYMENT APPLICATION **🎴 S&K GROCERY, INC.**

NAME: Dan King	JOB APPLYING FOR: _____

1. HOW DID YOU HEAR ABOUT THIS JOB? (PLEASE CHECK (✓) ALL APPROPRIATE BOXES.)

☐ FRIENDS   ☐ INTERNET JOB SITE   ☐ HELP WANTED SIGN

☐ JOB BOARD   ☐ CLASSIFIEDS   ☐ EMPLOYMENT AGENCY

2. HOURS: ☐ PART-TIME ☐ FULL-TIME

3. HAVE YOU HAD ANY EXPERIENCE? ☐ YES ☐ NO	IF YES, WHAT? WHEN? _____

4. REFERENCES: Lily Wong, Manager, Zhou Market

FOR OFFICE USE ONLY

RESUME RECEIVED: 9/17	INTERVIEWED BY: Ron Hill 9/21
HIRED? ☐ YES ☐ NO	WAGES:

2. **Look at page 6 and at Exercise 1. *True* or *False*?**

a. Dan filled out an application. _____true_____

b. Dan wrote a resume. _____

c. He didn't write a cover letter. _____

d. He sent in his resume before the interview. _____

e. He set up an interview for the job. _____

f. He went on an interview with Lily Wong at Zhou Market. _____

g. Dan didn't get hired. _____

3. **What about you? What do you think are the best ways to find a job? Number them in order. (1 = the best)**

____ look in the classifieds   ____ check Internet job sites

____ look for a help wanted sign   ____ go to an employment agency

____ network   ____ Other: _____

See page 166 for listening practice. **7**

A. Prepare for the interview.

B. Dress appropriately.

C. Be neat.

D. Bring your resume and ID.

E. Don't be late.

F. Be on time.

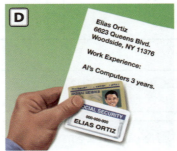

G. Turn off your cell phone.

H. Greet the interviewer.

I. Shake hands.

J. Make eye contact.

K. Listen carefully.

L. Talk about your experience.

M. Ask questions.

N. Thank the interviewer.

O. Write a thank-you note.

More vocabulary

benefits: health insurance, vacation pay, or other things the employer can offer an employee

inquire about benefits: ask about benefits

Think about it. Discuss.

1. How can you prepare for an interview?
2. Why is it important to make eye contact?
3. What kinds of questions should you ask?

1. **Look at page 8. When did Mr. Ortiz . . . ? Check (✓) the columns.**

	Before the Interview	During the Interview	After the Interview
a. ask questions		✓	
b. dress appropriately			
c. prepare			
d. talk about his experience			
e. shake hands			
f. greet the interviewer			
g. write a thank-you note			

2. **Look at the picture. Check (✓) Amy's interview skills.**

3. **What about you? Check (✓) the things you do on a job interview.**

Interview Skills Checklist

☐ be on time   ☐ bring resume   ☐ make eye contact

☐ dress appropriately ☐ bring ID   ☐ listen carefully

☐ be neat   ☐ turn off cell phone ☐ talk about job experience

See page 167 for listening practice.

A. **start** a conversation

B. **make** small talk

C. **compliment** someone

D. **offer** something

E. **thank** someone

F. **apologize**

G. **accept** an apology

H. **invite** someone

I. **accept** an invitation

J. **decline** an invitation

K. **agree**

L. **disagree**

M. **explain** something

N. **check** your understanding

More vocabulary

request: to ask for something
accept a compliment: to thank someone for a compliment

Pair practice. Follow the directions.

1. Start a conversation with your partner.
2. Make small talk with your partner.
3. Compliment each other.

1. Look at page 10. Circle the correct words.

a. | Hi. I'm Danny. | make small talk / (start a conversation)

b. | Is that *Donny*? | check your understanding / explain something

c. | Nice day, isn't it? | compliment someone / make small talk

d. | That's a nice jacket. | agree / compliment someone

e. | I'm having a party tonight. Please come. | accept an invitation / invite someone

2. Complete the conversations from Amy's party. Use the sentences in the box.

| This food is great! | ~~Coats go in there.~~ | Oh! Sorry! | There? |
| No. It's very bad! | Here's a napkin. | Thanks! | That's OK. |

a. *Coats go in there.*

b.

c.

d.

3. Look at Exercise 2. In which picture is someone . . . ?

1. accepting an apology   *c*   4. disagreeing   ____

2. apologizing   ____   5. offering something   ____

3. checking understanding   ____   6. thanking someone   ____

The Workplace

1. entrance

2. customer

3. office

4. employer / boss

5. receptionist

6. safety regulations

Listen and point. Take turns.
A: Point to the front entrance.
B: Point to the receptionist.
A: Point to the time clock.

Dictate to your partner. Take turns.
A: *Can you spell employer?*
B: *I'm not sure. Is it e-m-p-l-o-y-e-r?*
A: *Yes, that's right.*

7. time clock

8. supervisor

9. employee

10. payroll clerk

11. pay stub

12. wages

13. deductions

14. paycheck

PLEASE CLOCK IN AND OUT

EMPLOYEES ONLY

9:15

Fix this first.

OK.

IRINA'S COMPUTER SERVICE
7000 Main Street
Houston, TX 77031

10/17/11 to 10/23/11

Kate Babic
000-23-4567

Salary		**$ 800.00**
Deductions		
Federal	88.00	
State	22.40	
Social Security	51.00	
Medicare	12.00	
SDI	7.50	
Net		**$ 619.10**

IRINA'S COMPUTER SERVICE
7000 Main Street
Houston, TX 77031

Check number:
123456789 999999999 123

Pay to the order of _____ Kate Babic _____ $ 619.10

Six hundred nineteen and 10/100 dollars

Town Bank

Irina Jankov

Ways to talk about wages

I **earn** $250 a week.
He **makes** $7 an hour.
I'm **paid** $1,000 a month.

Role play. Talk to an employer.

A: *Is everything correct on your paycheck?*
B: *No, it isn't. I make $250 a week, not $200.*
A: *Let's talk to the payroll clerk. Where is she?*

The Workplace

1. Look at pages 12–13. *True* or *False*?

a. Irina Sarkov is the receptionist.   *false*

b. The receptionist sits across from the entrance.   _____

c. The time clock shows 9:15.   _____

d. The safety regulations are in the office.   _____

e. There are two employees in the office.   _____

f. The employer is writing paychecks now.   _____

g. A customer is at the entrance.   _____

h. The employer is also the owner.   _____

2. Who said . . . ? Use the words in the box.

| employee | ~~employer~~ | payroll clerk | receptionist | customer | supervisor |

a. My company is growing. I need to hire more employees.   *employer*

b. Great. Now, please do this next.   _____

c. Here's your paycheck for this week.   _____

d. Hello, this is R & M, Inc. Can I help you?   _____

e. I don't understand my pay stub.   _____

f. Something is wrong with my computer.   _____

3. **Look at pages 12–13. Circle the answers to complete the sentences.**

   a. (An employee) / The boss is fixing a computer.

   b. Kate Babic is talking to the payroll clerk / supervisor.

   c. Her deductions / wages are $800.

   d. Irina Sarkov's signature is on the paycheck / pay stub.

   e. The time clock is near the receptionist / entrance.

4. **Look at the pay stub. *True* or *False*?**

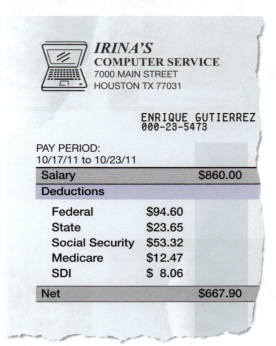

IRINA'S
COMPUTER SERVICE
7000 MAIN STREET
HOUSTON TX 77031

ENRIQUE GUTIERREZ
000-23-5473

PAY PERIOD:
10/17/11 to 10/23/11

Salary	$860.00
Deductions	
Federal	$94.60
State	$23.65
Social Security	$53.32
Medicare	$12.47
SDI	$ 8.06
Net	**$667.90**

   a. Irina is Enrique's supervisor.   *false*

   b. Enrique is an employee at Irina's Computer Service.   _____

   c. This pay stub is for one month.   _____

   d. His wages are $667.90 after deductions.   _____

   e. Enrique pays five different deductions.   _____

   f. The pay stub shows the office phone number.   _____

   g. The Social Security deduction is $8.06.   _____

See page 167 for listening practice.

Workplace Clothing

Construction Worker

Road Worker

Automotive Painter

Food Processor

1. hard hat

2. work shirt

3. tool belt

4. Hi-Visibility safety vest

5. work pants

6. steel toe boots

7. ventilation mask

8. coveralls

9. bump cap

10. safety glasses

11. apron

Manager

Salesperson

Farmworker

Ranch Hand

12. blazer

13. tie

14. polo shirt

15. name tag

16. bandana

17. work gloves

18. cowboy hat

19. jeans

Pair practice. Make new conversations.

A: *What do* <u>construction workers</u> *wear to work?*
B: *They wear* <u>hard hats</u> *and* <u>tool belts</u>.
A: *What do* <u>road workers</u> *wear to work?*

Use the new words.

Look at pages 154–155. Name the workplace clothing you see.

A: *He's wearing* <u>a hard hat</u>.
B: *She's wearing* <u>scrubs</u>.

16

Security Guard

Emergency Worker

Counterperson

Chef

Line Cook

20. security shirt

21. badge

22. security pants

23. helmet

24. jumpsuit

25. hairnet

26. smock

27. disposable gloves

28. chef's hat

29. chef's jacket

30. waist apron

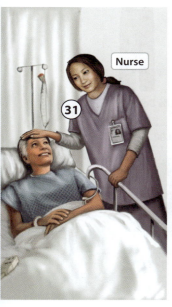

Nurse

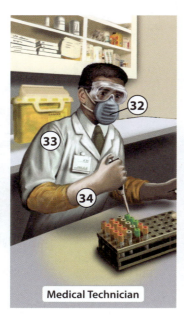

Medical Technician

O.R.

Surgeon

Surgical Assistant

31. scrubs

32. face mask

33. lab coat

34. latex gloves

35. surgical scrub cap

36. surgical mask

37. surgical gown

38. surgical scrubs

Ask your classmates. Share the answers.

1. Which of these outfits would you like to wear?
2. Which of these items are in your closet?
3. Do you wear safety clothing at work? What kinds?

Think about it. Discuss.

1. What other jobs require helmets? disposable gloves?
2. Is it better to have a uniform or wear your own clothes at work? Why?

Workplace Clothing

1. **Look at pages 16–17. Put the words in the correct column.**

For Your Head	For Your Face	For Your Hands
hard hat	_____	_____
_____	_____	_____
_____	_____	**For Your Feet**
_____		_____
_____		
_____		

2. **Look at the online catalog. Write the names of the workplace clothing. Use the words on the left side of the catalog page.**

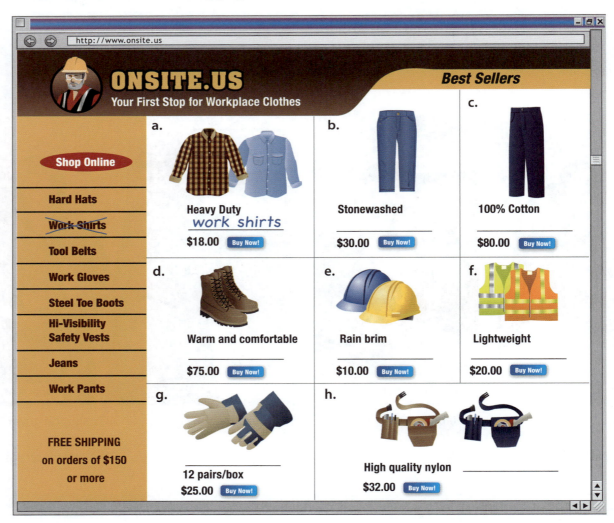

http://www.onsite.us

ONSITE.US
Your First Stop for Workplace Clothes

Best Sellers

Shop Online

Hard Hats
~~Work Shirts~~
Tool Belts
Work Gloves
Steel Toe Boots
Hi-Visibility Safety Vests
Jeans
Work Pants

FREE SHIPPING
on orders of $150
or more

a.
Heavy Duty
work shirts
$18.00 Buy Now!

b.
Stonewashed
_____
$30.00 Buy Now!

c.
100% Cotton
_____
$80.00 Buy Now!

d.
Warm and comfortable
_____
$75.00 Buy Now!

e.
Rain brim
_____
$10.00 Buy Now!

f.
Lightweight
_____
$20.00 Buy Now!

g.
12 pairs/box
$25.00 Buy Now!

h.
High quality nylon _____
$32.00 Buy Now!

3. **Look at pages 16–17. *True* or *False*? Correct the underlined words in the false sentences.**

a. The construction worker is wearing a ~~polo~~ *work* shirt.   <u>   *false*   </u>

b. The road worker is wearing <u>jeans</u>.   _____

c. The farmworker is wearing <u>work gloves</u>.   _____

d. The salesperson is wearing a <u>badge</u>.   _____

e. The manager is wearing a <u>blazer</u>.   _____

f. The counterperson is wearing a <u>chef's hat</u>.   _____

g. The nurse is wearing <u>scrubs</u>.   _____

h. The security guard has a <u>name tag</u>.   _____

i. The medical technician is wearing a <u>lab coat</u>.   _____

j. The surgeon is wearing a <u>surgical scrub cap</u>.   _____

4. **Look at the online catalog in Exercise 2. What items will people buy? Complete the chart.**

Job	Quantity	Item	Item Price	Total
a. road worker	2 pairs	<u>steel toe boots</u>	$75	<u>$150</u>
	1 pair	_____	$80	_____
b. construction worker	1	_____	$32	_____
	2	safety vests	_____	_____
	1 box	_____	_____	_____

5. **What about you? Check (✓) the clothing you have. Do you wear the clothing for work?**

		For Work	Not for Work
☐	safety glasses	☐	☐
☐	waist apron	☐	☐
☐	blazer	☐	☐
☐	polo shirt	☐	☐
☐	work gloves	☐	☐
☐	helmet	☐	☐
☐	hairnet	☐	☐

See page 168 for listening practice.   19

Safety Hazards and Hazardous Materials

1. careless worker
2. careful worker
3. poisonous fumes
4. broken equipment
5. frayed cord
6. slippery floor
7. radioactive materials
8. flammable liquids

Safety Equipment

9. hard hat
10. safety glasses
11. safety goggles
12. safety visor
13. respirator
14. particle mask
15. ear plugs
16. earmuffs
17. work gloves
18. back support belt
19. knee pads
20. safety boots
21. fire extinguisher
22. two-way radio

1. **Look at page 20. Match.**

1.   2.   3.   4. 5.

__3__ **a.** frayed cord   ____ **d.** flammable liquids

____ **b.** slippery floor   ____ **e.** radioactive materials

____ **c.** poisonous fumes

2. **Look at the worker. Check (✓) his safety equipment.**

Super Safe Sam

Job Safety
Better safe than sorry!

✓ back support belt	☐ respirator
☐ earmuffs	☐ safety boots
☐ ear plugs	☐ safety glasses
☐ fire extinguisher	☐ safety goggles
☐ hard hat	☐ safety visor
☐ knee pads	☐ two-way radio
☐ particle mask	☐ work gloves

3. **What about you? Which safety equipment do you use at work? At home? Write a list for each. Discuss your list with a classmate.**

At Work   At Home

_____   _____

_____   _____

_____   _____

_____   _____

_____   _____

See page 168 for listening practice.

A Hotel

1. doorman	4. concierge	7. bellhop	10. guest
2. revolving door	5. gift shop	8. luggage cart	11. desk clerk
3. parking attendant	6. bell captain	9. elevator	12. front desk

13. guest room	15. king-size bed	17. room service	19. housekeeping cart
14. double bed	16. suite	18. hallway	20. housekeeper

21. pool service	23. maintenance	25. meeting room
22. pool	24. gym	26. ballroom

1. Look at page 22. Circle the words to complete the sentences.

a. The ~~concierge~~ / parking attendant is on the phone.

b. The elevator is across from the gift shop / luggage cart.

c. One of the guest rooms has two double / king-size beds.

d. The housekeeping cart is in the hallway / ballroom.

e. Maintenance / The desk clerk is repairing the ice machine.

f. There are two bell captains / guests in the suite.

g. The doorman isn't opening the door / revolving door.

2. Look at the hotel directory in the guest room. What number do you call for . . . ?

HOTEL EDISON ☎ DIRECTORY

1 2 3 4 5 6 7 8

HOTEL EDISON

a. room service __3__

b. gift shop ____

c. pool ____

d. meeting room ____

e. front desk ____

f. housekeeper ____

g. bellhop ____

h. gym ____

3. What about you? Would you like to be a guest at the hotel in your dictionary?

☐ Yes   ☐ No   Why? _____

See page 168 for listening practice.

A. **dust** the furniture

B. **recycle** the newspapers

C. **clean** the oven

D. **mop** the floor

E. **polish** the furniture

F. **make** the bed

G. **put away** the toys

H. **vacuum** the carpet

I. **wash** the windows

J. **sweep** the floor

K. **scrub** the sink

L. **empty** the trash

M. **wash** the dishes

N. **dry** the dishes

O. **wipe** the counter

P. **change** the sheets

Q. **take out** the garbage

Pair practice. Make new conversations.

A: *Let's clean this place. First, I'll sweep the floor.*
B: *I'll mop the floor when you finish.*

Ask your classmates. Share the answers.

1. Who does the housework in your home?
2. How often do you wash the windows?
3. When should kids start to do housework?

1. **Look at page 24. What are the people doing? Circle the words.**

   a. "Can we do this with magazines, too?"   ~~recycling newspapers~~ / taking out the garbage

   b. "Dad, does this truck go here?"   dusting the furniture / putting away the toys

   c. "I like this new blanket."   making the bed / sweeping the floor

   d. "Is this the last plate, Dad?"   cleaning the oven / drying the dishes

2. **Look at the room. Check (✓) the *completed* jobs.**

To Do

   - ✓ wash the sheets
   - ☐ change the sheets
   - ☐ sweep the floor
   - ☐ empty the trash
   - ☐ polish the dresser
   - ☐ scrub the sink
   - ☐ mop the bathroom floor
   - ☐ take out the newspapers

3. **What about you? How often do you . . . ? Check (✓) the columns.**

	Every Day	Every Week	Every Month	Never
dust the furniture				
polish the furniture				
recycle the newspapers				
wash the dishes				
vacuum the carpet				
wipe the counter				
scrub the sink				
put away the toys				
Other: _____				

See page 169 for listening practice.

Cleaning Supplies

 1
 2
 3
 4
 5
 6

 7
 8
 9
 10
 11
 12

 13
 14
 15
 16
 17
 18

 19
 20
 21
 22
 23
 24

1. feather duster
2. recycling bin
3. oven cleaner
4. rubber gloves
5. steel-wool soap pads
6. sponge mop
7. bucket / pail
8. furniture polish

9. rags
10. vacuum cleaner
11. vacuum cleaner attachments
12. vacuum cleaner bag
13. stepladder
14. glass cleaner
15. squeegee
16. broom

17. dustpan
18. cleanser
19. sponge
20. scrub brush
21. dishwashing liquid
22. dish towel
23. disinfectant wipes
24. trash bags

Ways to ask for something

Please hand me <u>the squeegee</u>.
Can you get me <u>the broom</u>?
I need <u>the sponge mop</u>.

Pair practice. Make new conversations.

A: *Please hand me <u>the sponge mop</u>.*
B: *Here you go. Do you need <u>the bucket</u>?*
A: *Yes, please. Can you get me <u>the rubber gloves</u>, too?*

1. **Look at page 26. What can you use to clean the . . . ? There may be more correct answers than you can write here.**

Windows	Floor	Dishes
glass cleaner	_____	_____
_____	_____	_____
_____	_____	_____
_____	_____	_____
	_____	

2. **Match each item with the correct coupon.**

TO BUY

_4_ a. feather duster
___ b. steel-wool soap pads
___ c. sponges
___ d. pail
___ e. cleanser
___ f. trash bags
___ g. dishwashing liquid
___ h. rubber gloves
___ i. vacuum cleaner bags
___ j. disinfectant wipes

3. **What about you? Look at the cleaning supplies in Exercise 2. Which ones do you have? What do you use them for?**

Example: *feather duster—dust the desk*

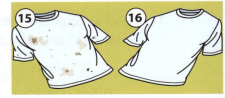

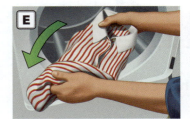

1. laundry
2. laundry basket
3. washer
4. dryer
5. dryer sheets

6. fabric softener
7. bleach
8. laundry detergent
9. clothesline
10. clothespin

11. hanger
12. spray starch
13. iron
14. ironing board
15. **dirty** T-shirt

16. **clean** T-shirt
17. **wet** shirt
18. **dry** shirt
19. **wrinkled** shirt
20. **ironed** shirt

A

A. **Sort** the laundry.

B

B. **Add** the detergent.

C

C. **Load** the washer.

D

D. **Clean** the lint trap.

E

E. **Unload** the dryer.

F

F. **Fold** the laundry.

G

G. **Iron** the clothes.

H

H. **Hang up** the clothes.

  wash in cold water

  line dry

  no bleach

  dry clean only, do not wash

Pair practice. Make new conversations.
A: *I have to <u>sort the laundry</u>. Can you help?*
B: *Sure. Here's <u>the laundry basket</u>.*
A: *Thanks a lot!*

1. **Look at page 28. Where is the . . . ? Use *in* or *on* in your answers.**

   a. iron   _on the ironing board_

   b. fabric softener   _____

   c. spray starch   _____

   d. wet polo shirt   _____

   e. laundry   _____

   f. clothespins   _____

2. **Look at the pictures. Write the instructions. Use the sentences in the box.**

Clean the lint trap.	Fold the laundry.	Unload the washer.
~~Sort the laundry.~~	Load the washer.	Add the detergent.

   a. _Sort the laundry._   b. _____   c. _____

   d. _____   e. _____   f. _____

3. **What about you? Do you do the laundry in your family? Check (✓) the items you use.**

   ☐ iron   ☐ hanger   ☐ clothespins

   ☐ ironing board   ☐ spray starch   ☐ dryer sheets

   ☐ clothesline   ☐ fabric softener   ☐ bleach

A Restaurant Kitchen

1. short-order cook	**3.** walk-in freezer	**5.** storeroom	**7.** head chef / executive che
2. dishwasher	**4.** food preparation worker	**6.** sous chef	

Restaurant Dining

8. server	**11.** maitre d'	**14.** banquet room
9. diner	**12.** headwaiter	**15.** runner
10. buffet	**13.** bus person	**16.** caterer

More vocabulary

line cook: short-order cook
wait staff: servers, headwaiters, and runners

Ask your classmates. Share the answers.

1. Have you ever worked in a hotel? What did you do?
2. What is the hardest job in a hotel?
3. Would you prefer to stay at a hotel in the city or in the country?

1. **Look at page 30. Who is . . . ?**

   a. leaving the walk-in freezer   _food preparation worker_

   b. washing dishes   _____

   c. sitting near the buffet   _____

   d. talking to the bus person   _____

   e. working in the banquet room   _____ and _____

   f. carrying food to a diner   _____

   g. seating a diner at a table   _____

2. **Look at page 30. Where are they? Check (✓) all the correct columns.**

	Dining Room	Banquet Room	Kitchen
a. servers	✓	✓	
b. diners			
c. short-order cook			
d. sous chef			
e. caterer			
f. bus person			
g. head chef			
h. maitre d'			
i. runner			

3. **Look at page 30. Who said . . . ?**

   a. Would you like a cup of coffee with that?   _server_

   b. The plates are all clean.   _____

   c. These two hamburgers are ready.   _____

   d. Thanks. The rolls look great.   _____

See page 170 for listening practice.

1. can opener	9. wooden spoon	17. colander	25. saucepan
2. grater	10. casserole dish	18. kitchen timer	26. cake pan
3. steamer	11. garlic press	19. spatula	27. cookie sheet
4. plastic storage container	12. carving knife	20. eggbeater	28. pie pan
5. frying pan	13. roasting pan	21. whisk	29. pot holders
6. pot	14. roasting rack	22. strainer	30. rolling pin
7. ladle	15. vegetable peeler	23. tongs	31. mixing bowl
8. double boiler	16. paring knife	24. lid	

Pair practice. Make new conversations.

A: *Please hand me the whisk.*
B: *Here's the whisk. Do you need anything else?*
A: *Yes, pass me the casserole dish.*

Use the new words.
Look at page 47. Name the kitchen utensils you see.

A: *Here's a grater.*
B: *This is a mixing bowl.*

1. **Look at page 32. *True* or *False*?**

   a. The grater is below the steamer and the plastic storage container. _____*false*_____

   b. The eggbeater is between the spatula and the whisk. _____

   c. The vegetable peeler, tongs, strainer, and saucepan are on the wall. _____

   d. The ladle and the wooden spoon are in the pot. _____

   e. There are lids on the double boiler and casserole dish. _____

   f. The frying pan is next to the roasting pan. _____

   g. The kitchen timer is near the colander and the paring knife. _____

2. **Complete the two-part words. Use the words in the box.**

bowl	holders	knife	opener
~~pan~~	pin	press	sheet

   a. cake _____*pan*_____

   b. mixing _____

   c. garlic _____

   d. pot _____

   e. rolling _____

   f. cookie _____

   g. can _____

   h. carving _____

3. **Which kitchen utensils do you need? Use words from Exercise 2.**

   a. _____*garlic press*_____

   b. _____

   c. _____

   d. _____

   e. _____

   f. _____

1. dining room
2. hostess
3. high chair
4. booth
5. to-go box
6. patron / diner
7. menu
8. server / waiter

A. **set** the table

B. **seat** the customer

C. **pour** the water

D. **order** from the menu

E. **take** the order

F. **serve** the meal

G. **clear** / **bus** the dishes

H. **carry** the tray

I. **pay** the check

J. **leave** a tip

More vocabulary

eat out: to go to a restaurant to eat
take out: to buy food at a restaurant and take it home to eat

Look at the pictures.
Describe what is happening.
A: *She's seating the customer*.
B: *He's taking the order*.

9. server / waitress

10. dessert tray

11. bread basket

12. busser

13. dish room

14. dishwasher

15. kitchen

16. chef

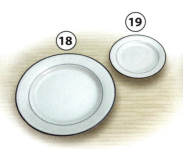
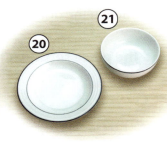

17. place setting

18. dinner plate

19. bread-and-butter plate

20. salad plate

21. soup bowl

22. water glass

23. wine glass

24. cup

25. saucer

26. napkin

27. salad fork

28. dinner fork

29. steak knife

30. knife

31. teaspoon

32. soupspoon

Pair practice. Make new conversations.

A: *Excuse me, this spoon is dirty.*
B: *I'm so sorry. I'll get you a clean spoon right away.*
A: *Thanks.*

Role play. Talk to a new busser.

A: *Do the salad forks go on the left?*
B: *Yes. They go next to the dinner forks.*
A: *What about the…?*

1. Look at pages 34–35. Who . . . ?

a. washes dishes   _dishwasher_

b. leaves a tip   _____

c. takes the orders   _____

d. cooks food   _____

e. seats the customers   _____

f. orders from the menu   _____

2. Look at pages 34–35. Circle the answers.

a. The patrons are in the dish room / (dining room).

b. The baby is in the booth / high chair.

c. The chef is in the dish room / kitchen.

d. The hostess is in the dining room / kitchen.

e. The server pours the water in the dish room / dining room.

3. Look at the order and the place setting. Check (✓) the items the diner needs.

GUEST CHECK

Date	Table	Guests	Server	
				410121

onion soup
house salad
steak
broccoli
mashed potatoes
garlic bread
half bottle of red wine
coffee

Total

Thank you! Please come again.

☐ dinner plate   ☐ wine glass   ☐ dinner fork

✓ salad plate   ☐ cup   ☐ steak knife

☐ soup bowl   ☐ saucer   ☐ knife

☐ bread-and-butter plate   ☐ napkin   ☐ teaspoon

☐ water glass   ☐ salad fork   ☐ soupspoon

4. Look at the menu. Complete the check.

The Bistro
MENU

Soup of the day	$4.50
House salad	$3.50
Fish of the day	$15.50
Chicken á l'orange	$12.50
Sirloin steak	$19.00
Vegetables	$2.50
Potatoes	$2.50
Cherry pie	$4.00
with ice cream	$5.00
Coconut cake	$4.50
Coffee or tea	$1.50

The Bistro
242 West Street   555-0700
GUEST CHECK

				832000

black bean soup	$4.50
house salad	_____
grilled salmon	_____
peas	_____
french fries	_____
cherry pie w/vanilla ice cream	_____
coffee	_____
Subtotal	_____
Tax (5%)	_____
Total	_____

THANK YOU!

5. In the United States, most restaurant patrons leave a tip for the server when they pay the check. The tip is often 15% of the subtotal. Look at the check in Exercise 4. Circle the answers and complete the sentences.

a. The subtotal is ___$35.00___ .   (**$35.00**) $36.75 $40.25

b. A 15% tip is _____ . $1.75 $5.25 $4.72

c. Diners leave the tip on the _____ .   menu   table   dinner plate

6. What about you? Do restaurant patrons leave tips for the server in your

native country? _____

If *yes*, how much? _____

Where do they leave it? _____

See page 170 for listening practice.

A Fast Food Restaurant

1. hamburger	7. nachos	13. ice-cream cone	19. plastic utensils
2. french fries	8. taco	14. milkshake	20. sugar substitute
3. cheeseburger	9. burrito	15. donut	21. ketchup
4. onion rings	10. pizza	16. muffin	22. mustard
5. chicken sandwich	11. soda	17. counterperson	23. mayonnaise
6. hot dog	12. iced tea	18. straw	24. salad bar

Grammar Point: yes/no questions (do)

Do you like hamburgers? Yes, I do.
Do you like nachos? No, I don't.

Think about it. Discuss.

1. Do you think that fast food is bad for people? Why or why not?
2. What fast foods do you have in your country?
3. Do you have a favorite fast food restaurant? Which one?

1. **Look at page 38. *True* or *False*? Correct the underlined words in the false sentences.**

   a. There are muffins and ~~onion rings~~ *donuts* on the counter.   _____false_____

   b. The restaurant has <u>pizza</u>.   _____

   c. The <u>counterperson</u> is talking to a woman.   _____

   d. The <u>plastic utensils</u> are next to the salad bar.   _____

   e. A woman is drinking <u>a milkshake</u> with a straw.   _____

   f. A man is using <u>sugar substitute</u>.   _____

2. **Look at the orders. Write the food.**

   a.

QUICK & TASTY RECEIPT
Chicken sandwich
Thank You

   b.

QUICK & TASTY RECEIPT
Thank You

3. **What about you? Look at the fast food at page 38. Tell a classmate your order.**

   Example: *I'd like a cheeseburger.*

See page 171 for listening practice.

A Coffee Shop Menu

1. bacon
2. sausage
3. hash browns
4. toast
5. English muffin
6. biscuits
7. pancakes
8. waffles
9. hot cereal

10. grilled cheese sandwich
11. pickle
12. club sandwich
13. spinach salad
14. chef's salad
15. dinner salad
16. soup
17. rolls
18. coleslaw
19. potato salad
20. pasta salad
21. fruit salad

BREAKFAST SPECIAL
Served 6 a.m. to 11 a.m.

Two egg omelet with one side

HONEY

JELLY

SYRUP

LUNCH
Served 11 a.m. to 2 p.m.
All sandwiches come with soup or salad

SIDE SALADS

SALAD DRESSINGS

Thousand Island   Ranch

Italian   Blue Cheese

Ways to order from a menu

I'd like <u>a grilled cheese sandwich</u>.
I'll have <u>a bowl of tomato soup</u>.
Could I get <u>the chef's salad</u> with <u>ranch dressing</u>?

Pair practice. Make conversations.

A: <u>I'd like a grilled cheese sandwich, please</u>.
B: Anything else for you?
A: Yes, I'll have <u>a bowl of tomato soup</u> with that.

DINNER

22. roast chicken
23. mashed potatoes
24. steak
25. baked potato
26. spaghetti
27. meatballs
28. garlic bread
29. grilled fish
30. rice
31. meatloaf
32. steamed vegetables

DESSERTS

33. layer cake
34. cheesecake
35. pie
36. mixed berries

BEVERAGES

37. coffee
38. decaf coffee
39. tea
40. herbal tea
41. cream
42. low-fat milk

Ask your classmates. Share the answers.

1. Do you prefer vegetable soup or chicken soup?
2. Do you prefer tea or coffee?
3. Which desserts on the menu do you like?

Role play. Order a dinner from the menu.

A: *Are you ready to order?*
B: *I think so. I'll have the roast chicken.*
A: *Would you also like…?*

A Coffee Shop Menu

1. **Look at pages 40–41. Complete the chart. Do not include sandwiches or salads.**

meat	vegetables	breads	hot beverages
bacon			

2. **Look at the ingredients. Write the food.**

a. _____*club sandwich*_____

b. _____

c. _____

d. _____

e. _____

f. _____

3. Cross out the word that doesn't belong.

a. Potatoes   baked potato   hash browns   mashed potatoes   ~~rice~~

b. Breads   garlic bread   roll   pie   toast

c. Beverages   soup   coffee   low-fat milk   tea

d. Breakfast food   biscuits   layer cake   pancakes   waffles

e. Side salads   chef's salad   coleslaw   pasta salad   potato salad

f. Desserts   cheesecake   layer cake   pie   hot cereal

4. Look at the food. Complete the orders.

a. FOOD ORDER FORM

roast chicken

Thank You!

b. FOOD ORDER FORM

Thank You!

5. What about you? What's your favorite . . . ?

soup _____   dessert _____   hot beverage _____

See page 171 for listening practice.

Food Safety

A. **clean**

B. **separate**

C. **cook**

D. **chill**

A — Clean counters!
20 SECONDS
Wash your hands!

B — Use separate cutting boards for vegetables and meat!

C — Cook to the right temperature!

D — Refrigerate leftovers quickly!

Ways to Serve Meat and Poultry

1. fried chicken

2. barbecued / grilled ribs

3. broiled steak

4. roasted turkey

5. boiled ham

6. stir-fried beef

Ways to Serve Eggs

7. scrambled eggs

8. hardboiled eggs

9. poached eggs

10. eggs sunny-side up

11. eggs over easy

12. omelet

Role play. Make new conversations.

A: *How do you like your eggs?*
B: *I like them <u>scrambled</u>. And you?*
A: *I like them <u>hardboiled</u>.*

Ask your classmates. Share the answers.

1. Do you use separate cutting boards?
2. What is your favorite way to serve meat? poultry?
3. What are healthy ways of preparing meat? poultry?

Cheesy Tofu Vegetable Casserole

A. **Preheat** the oven.

B. **Grease** a baking pan.

C. **Slice** the tofu.

D. **Steam** the broccoli.

E. **Saute** the mushrooms.

F. **Spoon** sauce on top.

G. **Grate** the cheese.

H. **Bake**.

Easy Chicken Soup

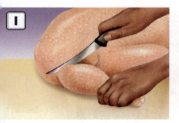

I. **Cut up** the chicken.

J. **Dice** the celery.

K. **Peel** the carrots.

L. **Chop** the onions.

M. **Boil** the chicken.

N. **Add** the vegetables.

O. **Stir**.

P. **Simmer**.

Quick and Easy Cake

Q. **Break** 2 eggs into a microwave-safe bowl.

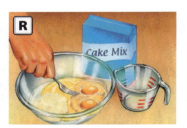

R. **Mix** the ingredients.

S. **Beat** the mixture.

T. **Microwave** for 5 minutes.

1. **Look at pages 44–45. *True* or *False*? Correct the underlined words in the false sentences.**

   counters
   a. Clean the kitchen ~~windows~~. _false_   d. Cook meat to 165°. _____

   b. Separate carrots and meat. _____   e. Chill leftovers in the refrigerator. _____

   c. Cook chicken to 160°. _____

2. **Look at the pictures. Which preparation has the most calories? Number them in order. (1 = the most calories)**

Calories in 3 oz. Chicken Breast

150   161   222

172   168   175

   ____ **a.** boiled   ____ **c.** grilled   _1_ **e.** fried

   ____ **b.** broiled   ____ **d.** roasted   ____ **f.** stir-fried

3. **What about you? Label the preparations and check (✓) the ways you like to eat eggs.**

   a.  _____ ☐   **b.**  _____ ☐

   c.   _____ ☐   **d.**    _____ ☐

   e.    _____ ☐   **f.**   _____ ☐

4. Look at pages 44–45. Read the recipe. <u>Underline</u> all the food preparation words.

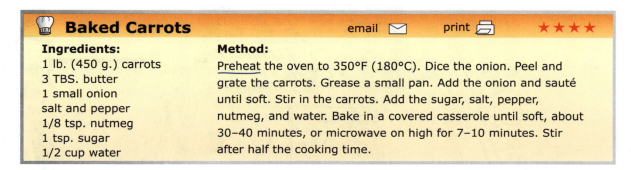

🧑‍🍳 **Baked Carrots**   email ✉   print 🖨   ★ ★ ★ ★

Ingredients:
1 lb. (450 g.) carrots
3 TBS. butter
1 small onion
salt and pepper
1/8 tsp. nutmeg
1 tsp. sugar
1/2 cup water

Method:
Preheat the oven to 350°F (180°C). Dice the onion. Peel and grate the carrots. Grease a small pan. Add the onion and sauté until soft. Stir in the carrots. Add the sugar, salt, pepper, nutmeg, and water. Bake in a covered casserole until soft, about 30–40 minutes, or microwave on high for 7–10 minutes. Stir after half the cooking time.

5. Look at the recipe in Exercise 4. Number the pictures in order.

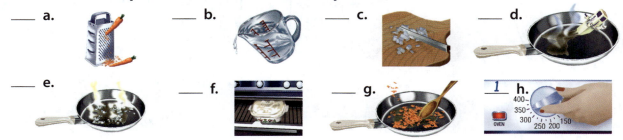

___ a.   ___ b.   ___ c.   ___ d.

___ e.   ___ f.   ___ g.   1 h.

6. Look at the pictures. Circle the words to complete the recipe.

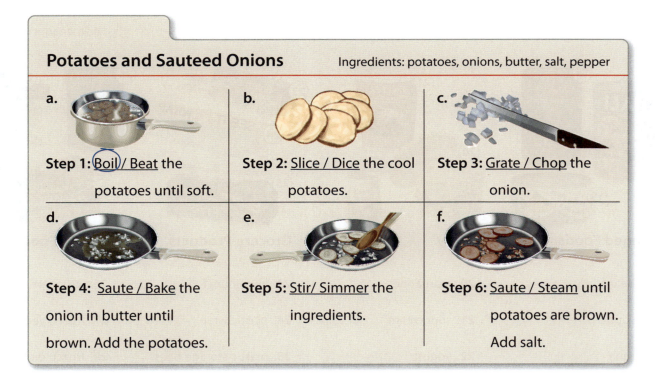

Potatoes and Sauteed Onions   Ingredients: potatoes, onions, butter, salt, pepper

a. Step 1: (Boil) / Beat the potatoes until soft.

b. Step 2: Slice / Dice the cool potatoes.

c. Step 3: Grate / Chop the onion.

d. Step 4: Saute / Bake the onion in butter until brown. Add the potatoes.

e. Step 5: Stir / Simmer the ingredients.

f. Step 6: Saute / Steam until potatoes are brown. Add salt.

See page 172 for listening practice. 🔵 **47**

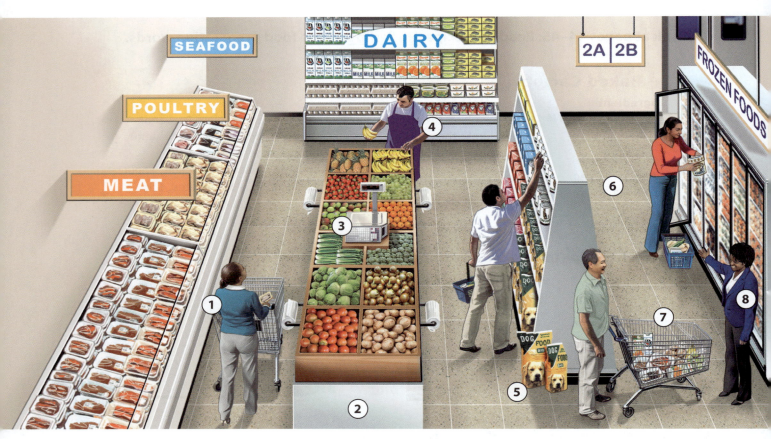

SEAFOOD

DAIRY

POULTRY

MEAT

2A | 2B

FROZEN FOODS

1. customer
2. produce section
3. scale
4. grocery clerk
5. pet food
6. aisle
7. cart
8. manager

Canned Foods

17. beans
18. soup
19. tuna

Dairy

20. margarine
21. sour cream
22. yogurt

Grocery Products

23. aluminum foil
24. plastic wrap
25. plastic storage bags

Frozen Foods

26. ice cream
27. frozen vegetables
28. frozen dinner

Ways to ask for information in a grocery store

Excuse me, where are the carrots?
Can you please tell me where to find the dog food?
Do you have any lamb chops today?

Pair practice. Make conversations.

A: *Can you please tell me where to find the dog food?*
B: *Sure. It's in aisle 1B. Do you need anything else?*
A: *Yes, where are the carrots?*

BAKERY

Best Baked Goods

15 items or less

Cash for Bottles | Cash for Bottle

IN | OUT

3A | 3B

SNACKS

9. shopping basket	**11.** line	**13.** cashier	**15.** cash register
10. self-checkout	**12.** checkstand	**14.** bagger	**16.** bottle return

WHOLE WHEAT

J&G

Franco's

Italian Roast

Tasty Cola

Baked not Fried!

YUM! CHOCOLATE

Baking Products

29. flour

30. sugar

31. oil

Beverages

32. apple juice

33. coffee

34. soda / pop

Snack Foods

35. potato chips

36. nuts

37. candy bar

Baked Goods

38. cookies

39. cake

40. bagels

Ask your classmates. Share the answers.

1. What is your favorite grocery store?

2. Do you prefer to shop alone or with friends?

3. Which foods from your country are hard to find?

Think about it. Discuss.

1. Is it better to shop every day or once a week? Why?

2. Why do grocery stores put snacks near the checkstands?

3. What's good and what's bad about small grocery stores?

1. **Look at pages 48–49.** *True* or *False*?

   a. A customer is buying pet food.   _____true_____

   b. The manager is in aisle 3A.   _____

   c. The grocery clerk is in the produce section.   _____

   d. There's a scale in the dairy section.   _____

   e. There are five customers in line.   _____

   f. You can get frozen vegetables in aisle 2B.   _____

   g. The bagger is near the cashier.   _____

   h. The self-checkout doesn't have a cash register.   _____

2. **Complete the conversations. Use the words in the box.**

~~Bagger~~	bottle return	cart	checkstands
~~Customer~~	manager	scale	self-checkout

  Customer : Excuse me. Where do I take these empty soda bottles?
      a.

Grocery Clerk: To the _____. Near aisle 1.
             b.

Amy: I'll get a shopping basket.

Jason: Get a _____. We have a lot on our list!
          c.

Jason: We need two pounds of potatoes. Is this enough?

Amy: There's a _____ over there. We can weigh them.
           d.

Jason: Look at the dates on these frozen dinners.

Amy: They're all too old. Let's tell the _____.
                  e.

Amy: Wow! Look at the lines at the _____.
                 f.

Jason: I see. But I don't like to use the _____. I like to talk to a person.
                      g.

Amy: Can we have four bags, please?

_____: Sure. Paper or plastic?
   h.

3. Look at the things Amy and Jason bought. Check (✓) the items on the shopping list.

Grocery List

☑ potatoes	☐ soup	☐ plastic wrap
☐ tuna	☐ cookies	☐ apple juice
☐ aluminum foil	☐ nuts	☐ sour cream
☐ bagels	☐ margarine	☐ coffee
☐ yogurt	☐ sugar	☐ cake
☐ potato chips	☐ ice cream	☐ candy bars
☐ beans	☐ oil	

4. Put the items from the list in Exercise 3 in the correct category. Use your dictionary for help.

Canned Foods	Dairy	Snack Foods
_____	_____	_____
_____	_____	_____
_____	_____	_____

Baking Products	Beverages	Baked Goods
_____	_____	_____
_____	_____	_____
		_____

Grocery Products	Produce	Frozen Foods
_____	*potatoes*	_____
_____		

See page 172 for listening practice.

Fish

1. trout
2. catfish
3. whole salmon
4. salmon steak
5. swordfish

6. halibut steak
7. tuna
8. cod

Shellfish

9. crab
10. lobster
11. shrimp
12. scallops
13. mussels

14. oysters
15. clams
16. **fresh** fish
17. **frozen** fish

18. white bread
19. wheat bread
20. rye bread

21. roast beef
22. corned beef
23. pastrami

24. salami
25. smoked turkey
26. American cheese

27. Swiss cheese
28. cheddar cheese
29. mozzarella cheese

Ways to order at the counter
I'd like some <u>roast beef</u>.
I'll have <u>a halibut steak</u> and some <u>shrimp</u>.
Could I get some <u>Swiss cheese</u>?

Pair practice. Make new conversations.
A: *What can I get for you?*
B: *<u>I'd like some roast beef</u>. How about a pound?*
A: *A pound of <u>roast beef</u> coming up!*

1. **Look at page 52. Write the names of the seafood.**

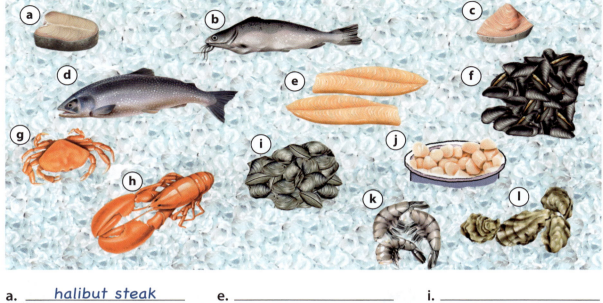

a. _halibut steak_   e. _____   i. _____

b. _____   f. _____   j. _____

c. _____   g. _____   k. _____

d. _____   h. _____   l. _____

2. **Look at the sandwich. Complete the order form. Check (✓) the correct boxes.**

Sandwich Order		
Meat	**Cheese**	**Bread**
✓ smoked turkey	☐ American	☐ white
☐ roast beef	☐ mozzarella	☐ wheat
☐ corned beef	☐ Swiss	☐ rye
☐ salami	☐ cheddar	
☐ pastrami		

3. **What about you? Complete your order with the food on the form in Exercise 2.**

I'd like a _____ sandwich with _____ cheese on _____ bread.

See page 173 for listening practice.

Containers and Packaging

1. bottles
2. jars
3. cans
4. cartons
5. containers
6. boxes

7. bags
8. packages
9. six-packs
10. loaves
11. rolls
12. tubes

13. a bottle of water
14. a jar of jam
15. a can of beans
16. a carton of eggs

17. a container of cottage cheese
18. a box of cereal
19. a bag of flour
20. a package of cookies

21. a six-pack of soda (pop)
22. a loaf of bread
23. a roll of paper towels
24. a tube of toothpaste

Grammar Point: count and non-count

Some foods can be counted: *an apple, two apples*.
Some foods can't be counted: *some rice, some water*.
For non-count foods, count containers: *two bags of rice*.

Pair practice. Make conversations.

A: *How many* <u>boxes of cereal</u> *do we need?*
B: *We need* <u>two boxes</u>.

1. Look at page 54. What is the container or packaging for . . . ?

a. pinto beans _____can_____   c. sour cream _____

b. plastic storage bags _____   d. potato chips _____

2. Complete these coupons. Use the words in the box.

bag	bottle	carton	loaf
six-pack	package	roll	~~tube~~

a.

2/$3 **Bright's toothpaste**

8.5 oz.

_____

Limit 2 *tube*

b.

BUY ONE GET ONE FREE.

Smart's Potato Chips, low salt

7 oz. _____

Limit 1 free item

c.

Special!

64 oz. orange juice

$3.10 / _____

d.

$1.99 **Stop and Save rye bread**

16 oz. _____

Limit 1 per customer

e.

SAVE 50 cents

Cola

one _____

Regular or diet

f.

SPECIAL! Chip's cookies (all varieties)

12-16 oz. _____

$2.99

g.

BUY ONE GET ONE FREE.

Maine Spring Water

16.9 oz. _____

h.

55 sq. ft _____

Strongy Paper Towels

3/$2.99

3. Write a shopping list. Use all the coupons in Exercise 2.

Example: *2 tubes of toothpaste*

See page 173 for listening practice.

Weights and Measurements

A. Measure the ingredients.

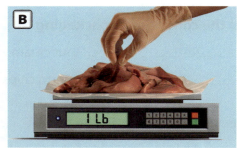

B. Weigh the food.

1 cup = 237 milliliters

C. Convert the measurements.

Liquid Measures

① 1 fl. oz.

② 1 c.

③ 1 pt.

④ 1 qt.

⑤ 1 gal.

Dry Measures

⑥ 1 tsp.

⑦ 1 TBS.

⑧ 1/4 c.

⑨ 1/2 c.

⑩ 1 c.

Weight

⑪

⑫

1. a fluid ounce of milk
2. a cup of oil
3. a pint of frozen yogurt
4. a quart of milk

5. a gallon of water
6. a teaspoon of salt
7. a tablespoon of sugar
8. a quarter cup of brown sugar

9. a half cup of raisins
10. a cup of flour
11. an ounce of cheese
12. a pound of roast beef

Equivalencies			Volume	Weight
3 tsp. = 1 TBS.	2 c. = 1 pt.		1 fl. oz. = 30 ml	1 oz. = 28.35 grams (g)
2 TBS. = 1 fl. oz.	2 pt. = 1 qt.		1 c. = 237 ml	1 lb. = 453.6 g
8 fl. oz. = 1 c.	4 qt. = 1 gal.		1 pt. = .47 L	2.205 lbs. = 1 kilogram (kg)
			1 qt. = .95 L	1 lb. = 16 oz.
			1 gal. = 3.79 L	

1. Look at page 56. Write the words.

a. oz. _____ounce_____

b. lb. _____

c. pt. _____

d. qt. _____

e. c. _____

f. tsp. _____

g. TBS. _____

h. gal. _____

2. Write the weight or measurement.

a. _____1 1/2 pounds of potatoes_____

b. _____

c. _____

d. _____

e. _____

f. _____

3. What about you? How much . . . do you eat or drink every week?

a. cheese _____

b. water _____

c. fish _____

d. sugar _____

See page 174 for listening practice.

1. music store
2. jewelry store
3. nail salon
4. bookstore

5. toy store
6. pet store
7. card store
8. florist

9. optician
10. shoe store
11. play area
12. guest services

More vocabulary
beauty shop: hair salon
men's store: men's clothing store
gift shop: a store that sells t-shirts, mugs, and other small gifts

Pair practice. Make new conversations.
A: *Where is the florist?*
B: *It's on the first floor, next to the optician.*

13. department store	**17.** candy store	**21.** elevator
14. travel agency	**18.** hair salon	**22.** cell phone kiosk
15. food court	**19.** maternity store	**23.** escalator
16. ice cream shop	**20.** electronics store	**24.** directory

Ways to talk about plans

Let's go to the <u>card store</u>.
I have to go to the <u>card store</u>.
I want to go to the <u>card store</u>.

Role play. Talk to a friend at the mall.

A: *Let's go to the <u>card store</u>. I need to buy <u>a card</u> for*
<u>Maggie's birthday</u>.
B: *OK, but can we go to the <u>shoe store</u> next?*

1. **Look at pages 58–59. Complete the mall directory. Use the words in the box.**

florist	jewelry store	nail salon	food court
travel agency	maternity store	hair salon	candy store
~~cell phone kiosk~~	ice cream shop	optician	~~pet store~~
toy store	electronics store	music store	shoe store

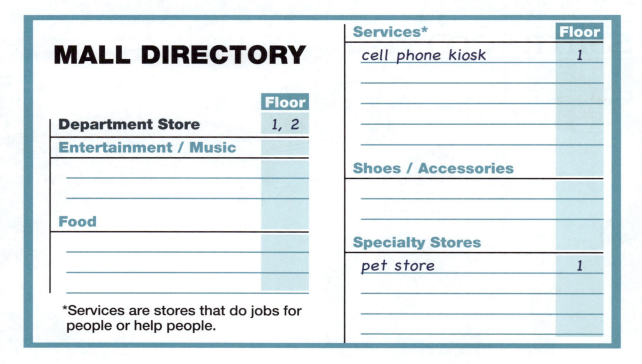

MALL DIRECTORY

Department Store	Floor
Department Store	1, 2
Entertainment / Music	
Food	

Services*	Floor
cell phone kiosk	1
Shoes / Accessories	
Specialty Stores	
pet store	1

*Services are stores that do jobs for people or help people.

2. **Look at the mall directory in Exercise 1. Where can you buy these items (other than a department store)?**

a. _____optician_____   b. _____   c. _____

d. _____   e. _____   f. _____

g. _____   h. _____   i. _____

3. **Look at this mall directory and map. Circle the words to complete the conversations.**

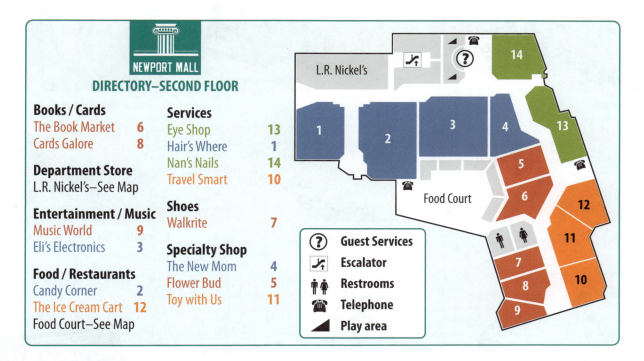

Customer 1: Excuse me. Where's the card store?

Guest Services: It's next to the <u>nail salon / (shoe store)</u>.
　　　　　　　　　　　　　　　　　a.

Customer 2: Can you tell me where the hair salon is?

Guest Services: Sure. It's across from <u>the department store / guest services</u>.
　　　　　　　　　　　　　　　　　　　　　　　b.

Customer 3: I'm looking for the <u>elevator / escalator</u>.
　　　　　　　　　　　　　　　　　　c.

Guest Services: It's next to Nickel's.

Customer 4: Hi. Where's the travel agency, please?

Guest Services: It's right over there. Next to the <u>toy / music</u> store.
　　　　　　　　　　　　　　　　　　　　　　d.

Customer 5: Excuse me. I'm looking for the candy store.

Guest Services: It's between the <u>music / electronics</u> store and the
　　　　　　　　　　　　　　　　　　　e.

　　　　　　　　　 <u>hair salon / maternity store</u>.
　　　　　　　　　　　　　　f.

Customer 6: Excuse me. Is there an optician in this mall?

Guest Services: Yes. There's one across from the <u>florist / bookstore</u>.
　　　　　　　　　　　　　　　　　　　　　　g.

See page 174 for listening practice.

Shopping

Ways to Pay

A. pay cash

B. use a credit card

C. use a debit card

D. write a (personal) check

E. use a gift card

F. cash a traveler's check

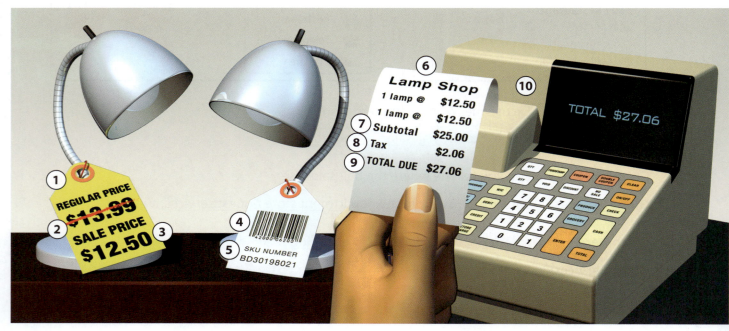

1. price tag
2. regular price
3. sale price
4. bar code
5. SKU number
6. receipt
7. price / cost
8. sales tax
9. total
10. cash register

G. buy / pay for

H. return

I. exchange

1. Look at page 62. Match.

1.

2.

3.

4.

5.

6.

__3__ **a.** SKU number ____ **c.** use a debit card ____ **e.** sales tax

____ **b.** bar code ____ **d.** use a gift card ____ **f.** regular price

2. Complete the shopping tips. Use the words in the box.

~~cash register~~	credit	debit	exchange	pay	total
price	price tag	receipt	return	sales	

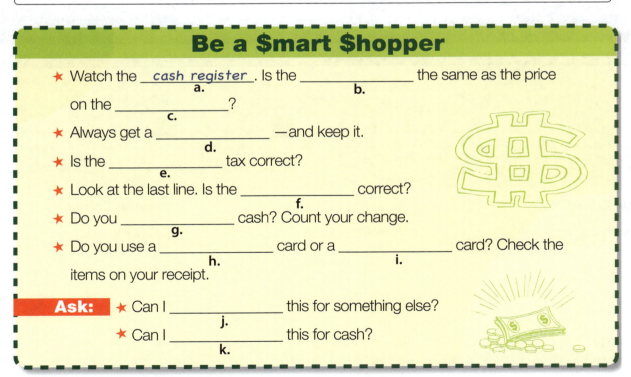

Be a $mart $hopper

★ Watch the ___cash register___. Is the _____ the same as the price
     a.   **b.**
   on the _____?
             c.

★ Always get a _____ —and keep it.
             d.

★ Is the _____ tax correct?
        e.

★ Look at the last line. Is the _____ correct?
                          f.

★ Do you _____ cash? Count your change.
          g.

★ Do you use a _____ card or a _____ card? Check the
               h.   **i.**
   items on your receipt.

Ask: ★ Can I _____ this for something else?
               j.

       ★ Can I _____ this for cash?
                  k.

3. What about you? What has sales tax in your state? How much is it?

See page 174 for listening practice.

Basic Colors

1. red

2. yellow

3. blue

4. orange

5. green

6. purple

7. pink

8. violet

9. turquoise

10. dark blue

11. light blue

12. bright blue

Neutral Colors

13. black

14. white

15. gray

16. cream / ivory

17. brown

18. beige / tan

Ask your classmates. Share the answers.
1. What colors are you wearing today?
2. What colors do you like?
3. Is there a color you don't like? What is it?

Use the new words. Look at pages 68–69.
Take turns naming the colors you see.
A: *His shirt is <u>blue</u>.*
B: *Her shoes are <u>white</u>.*

1. Look at the bar graph. Put the colors in order. (1 = favorite)

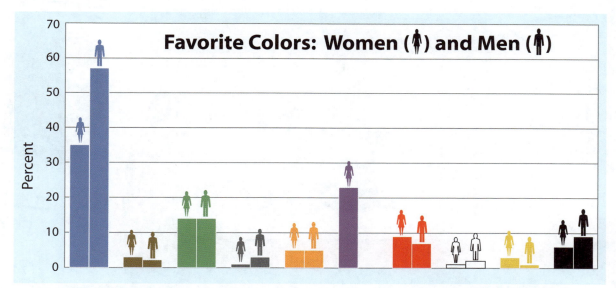

Based on information from: Hallock, Joe (2003) "Female Favorite Color Pie Chart" and "Male Favorite Color Pie Chart." http://www.joehallock.com/edu/com498/preferences.html

Women's Favorite Colors	Men's Favorite Colors
1. _____blue_____	1. _____
2. _____	2. _____
3. _____	3. _____
4. _____	4. _____
5. _____	5. _____
6. _____	6. _____
7. _____ and _____	7. _____ and _____
8. _____ and _____	8. _____

2. What about you? Put the colors in order. (1 = your favorite)

___ red   ___ turquoise   ___ yellow   ___ pink   ___ violet

___ brown   ___ light blue   ___ dark blue   ___ orange   ___ beige

See page 175 for listening practice.

1. The yellow sweaters are **on the left**.

2. The purple sweaters are **in the middle**.

3. The brown sweaters are **on the right**.

4. The red sweaters are **above** the blue sweaters.

5. The blue sweaters are **below** the red sweaters.

6. The turquoise sweater is **in** the box.

7. The white sweater is **in front of** the black sweater.

8. The black sweater is **behind** the white sweater.

9. The violet sweater is **next to** the gray sweater.

10. The gray sweater is **under** the orange sweater.

11. The orange sweater is **on** the gray sweater.

12. The green sweater is **between** the pink sweaters.

More vocabulary

near: in the same area
far from: not near

Role play. Make new conversations.

A: *Excuse me. Where are the red sweaters?*
B: *They're on the left, above the blue sweaters.*
A: *Thanks very much.*

1. **Look at page 66. *True* or *False*?**

   a. The red sweaters are above the yellow sweaters.   _____true_____

   b. The purple sweaters are next to the orange sweaters.   _____

   c. The white sweaters are between the black and gray sweaters.   _____

   d. The brown sweaters are on the left.   _____

   e. The dark blue sweaters are below the turquoise sweaters.   _____

2. **Follow the instructions below.**

   a. Put the letter **W** in the pink box.

   b. Put a **Y** below it.

   c. Put an **E** in the yellow box.

   d. Put an **I** above the **E**.

   e. Put a **P** next to the **E**, on the left.

   f. Put a **U** in the green box.

   g. Put an **O** between the **Y** and the **U**.

   h. Put an **E** above the **U**.

   i. Put an **R** next to the **U**, on the right.

   j. Put an **H** between the **W** and the **E**.

   k. Put the letters **E, N, R,** and **S** in the correct boxes to complete the question.

3. **What about you? Look at Exercise 2. Answer the question.**

   _____

See page 175 for listening practice.

Everyday Clothes

1. shirt

2. jeans

3. dress

4. T-shirt

5. baseball cap

6. socks

7. athletic shoes

A. **tie**

BEST OF JAZZ CONCERT

TICKETS

BEST OF JAZZ

Listen and point. Take turns.
A: *Point to the dress.*
B: *Point to the T-shirt.*
A: *Point to the baseball cap.*

Dictate to your partner. Take turns.
A: *Write dress.*
B: *Is that spelled d-r-e-s-s?*
A: *Yes. That's right.*

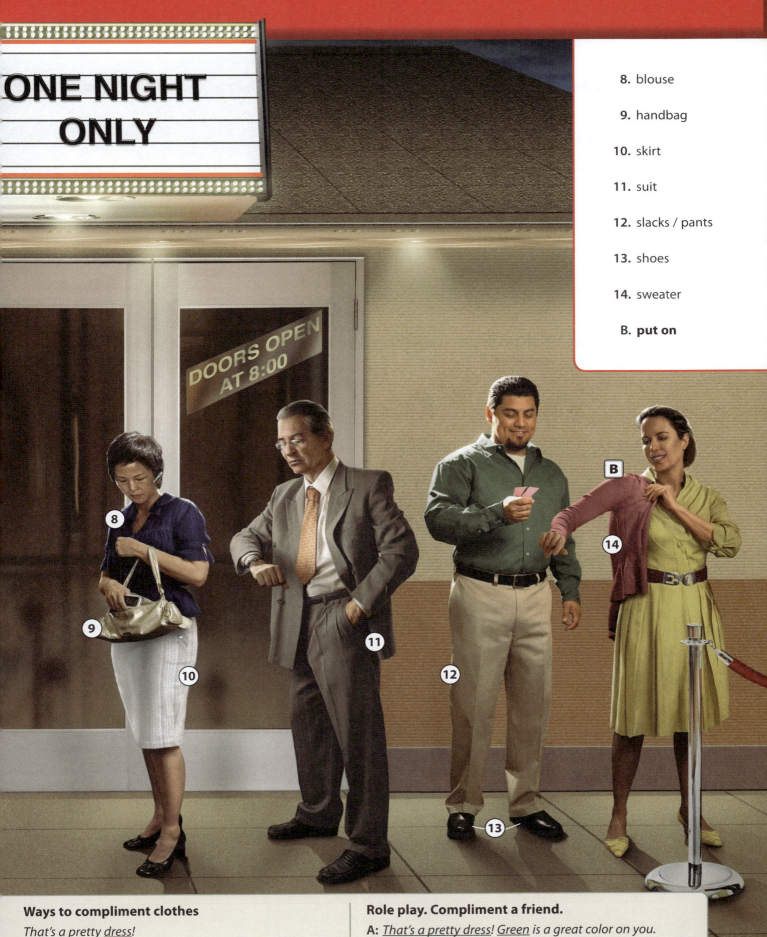

8. blouse

9. handbag

10. skirt

11. suit

12. slacks / pants

13. shoes

14. sweater

B. **put on**

Ways to compliment clothes

That's a pretty dress!

Those are great shoes!

I really like your baseball cap!

Role play. Compliment a friend.

A: *That's a pretty dress! Green is a great color on you.*

B: *Thanks! I really like your…*

1. Look at pages 68–69. Which clothing items are . . . ?

a. green ___*dress*___ and _____

b. dark blue _____, _____, and _____

c. red _____

d. yellow _____ and _____

e. white _____, _____, _____, _____, and _____

f. pink _____

g. orange _____

h. beige _____

2. Look at the picture of Courtney and Nicholas. Read the school clothing rules. Complete the sentences.

Courtney   Nicholas

CLOTHING RULES

Wear…	Don't wear…
shirts	T-shirts
blouses	jeans
slacks	baseball caps
skirts	athletic shoes
dresses	
socks	

What's OK?

a. Courtney is wearing a ___*blouse*___.

b. Nicholas is wearing _____.

c. He's also wearing _____.

What's NOT OK?

d. Courtney is wearing _____ and _____.

e. Nicholas is wearing a _____ and a _____.

3. What about you? What are you wearing today?

_____

4. **Look at pages 68–69.** *True* or *False*?

a. The man in the blue shirt is wearing jeans. _____true_____

b. The woman with white shoes is wearing socks. _____

c. The girl with the baseball cap is tying her shoes. _____

d. The woman in the skirt is putting on a sweater. _____

e. The woman with the sweater has a handbag. _____

f. The man in the green shirt and slacks has tickets. _____

5. **Look at pages 68–69. Circle the words to complete the conversation.**

Nina: Clio? I'm in front of the theater. Where are you? It's 7:45!

Clio: Sorry. I'm still getting dressed. What are you wearing?

Nina: A blue (blouse)/ T-shirt and a white <u>baseball cap / skirt</u>.
                     a.   **b.**

Clio: Is it cold out? Do I need a <u>handbag / sweater</u>?
                                       c.

Nina: Maybe. It *is* a little cool. What are you wearing?

Clio: Right now I'm wearing <u>a dress / pants</u>, but maybe I'll put on <u>slacks / socks</u>.
                                        d.   **e.**

Nina: OK. But hurry! The concert starts at 8:15!

6. **Cross out the word that doesn't belong.**

a. You wear it on top.	~~handbag~~	T-shirt	sweater
b. They're for your feet.	shoes	socks	pants
c. It's only for women.	dress	blouse	suit
d. You wear it on bottom.	jeans	shirt	slacks

7. **What about you? Complete the checklist. Do you wear . . . ?**

	Yes	No	If *yes*, where?
jeans	☐	☐	_____
athletic shoes	☐	☐	_____
a T-shirt	☐	☐	_____
a suit	☐	☐	_____
a sweater	☐	☐	_____
a baseball cap	☐	☐	_____

See page 175 for listening practice.

Casual, Work, and Formal Clothes

Casual Clothes

1. cap
2. cardigan sweater
3. pullover sweater
4. sports shirt
5. maternity dress

6. overalls
7. knit top
8. capris
9. sandals

Work Clothes

10. uniform
11. business suit
12. tie
13. briefcase

More vocabulary

three piece suit: matching jacket, vest, and slacks
outfit: clothes that look nice together
in fashion / in style: clothes that are popular now

Describe the people. Take turns.

A: *She's wearing a maternity dress.*
B: *He's wearing a uniform.*

Tran
Wedding

Formal Clothes

14. sports jacket / sports coat

15. vest

16. bow tie

17. tuxedo

18. evening gown

19. clutch bag

20. cocktail dress

21. high heels

Exercise Wear

22. sweatshirt / hoodie

23. sweatpants

24. tank top

25. shorts

Ask your classmates. Share the answers.

1. What's your favorite outfit?
2. Do you like to wear formal clothes? Why or why not?
3. Do you prefer to exercise in shorts or sweatpants?

Think about it. Discuss.

1. What jobs require formal clothes? Uniforms?
2. What's good and bad about wearing school uniforms?
3. What is your opinion of today's popular clothing?

Casual, Work, and Formal Clothes

1. **Look at pages 72–73. Circle the words to complete the sentences.**

   a. The woman's (business suit) / briefcase is purple.

   b. The cardigan / pullover sweater is green.

   c. The evening gown / uniform is turquoise.

   d. The tank top / sweatshirt is gray.

   e. The overalls / sweatpants are red.

   f. The knit top / sports shirt is blue and white.

   g. The cocktail / maternity dress is orange.

2. **Which clothes do women or men usually wear? Which clothes can both wear? Put the words from the box in the correct spaces in the circles.**

~~business suit~~	vest	shorts	cardigan sweater
uniform	tie	evening gown	sweatpants
pullover sweater	sandals	sports jacket	tuxedo
maternity dress	tank top	cocktail dress	capris

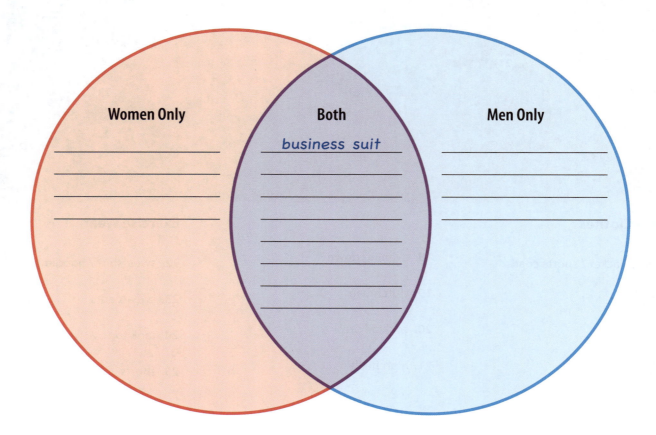

74

3. Look at the picture. Write the names of the clothing items on the list. Write the color, too.

Packing Log

to pack for *Chicago Wedding*

a *yellow tank top*
and _____

b _____
and _____

c _____
and _____

d _____
and _____

4. Match the activity with the clothes from Exercise 3.

HOTEL CHICAGO
ALEXANDRA PLACE
CHICAGO

SATURDAY

_c_ 1. Meet Nina in exercise room   7:30 a.m.
___ 2. Lunch near swimming pool   12:00 p.m.
___ 3. Formal dinner at the Grill   6:00 p.m.
___ 4. Wedding party at the   9:00 p.m.
     Grand Hotel Ballroom

5. What about you? Where do you wear these clothes? Check (✓) the columns.

	At School	At Work	At Home	At a Party	Never
pullover sweater					
vest					
sweatpants					
tuxedo or gown					
uniform					
cap					

See page 176 for listening practice.

Seasonal Clothing

1. hat
2. (over)coat
3. headband
4. leather jacket

5. winter scarf
6. gloves
7. headwrap
8. jacket

9. parka
10. mittens
11. ski hat
12. leggings

13. earmuffs
14. down vest
15. ski mask
16. down jacket

17. umbrella
18. raincoat
19. poncho

20. rain boots
21. trench coat

22. swimming trunks
23. straw hat
24. windbreaker

25. cover-up
26. swimsuit / bathing suit
27. sunglasses

Grammar Point: *should*

*It's raining. You **should** take an umbrella.*
*It's snowing. You **should** wear a scarf.*
*It's sunny. You **should** wear a straw hat.*

Pair practice. Make new conversations.

A: *It's <u>snowing</u>. You should wear <u>a scarf</u>.*
B: *Don't worry. I'm wearing my <u>parka</u>.*
A: *Good, and don't forget your <u>mittens</u>.*

1. **Look at page 76.** *True* or *False*?

    a. The man with the headwrap is wearing a jacket.   _____true_____

    b. The man with the down jacket is wearing earmuffs.   _____

    c. The woman in the poncho is wearing yellow rain boots.   _____

    d. The man with sunglasses is wearing a trench coat.   _____

2. **Look at the ad. Circle the words to complete the sentences.**

Dress for the Snow

Jessica is wearing a dark green <u>down vest</u> / (parka,)
                                                 a.

white <u>earmuffs</u> / <u>headband</u>, and green
                b.

<u>gloves</u> / <u>mittens</u>. Justin is wearing a blue
       c.

<u>down jacket</u> / <u>coat</u>, black <u>ski hat</u> / <u>ski mask</u>, and
         d.   **e.**

a light blue <u>winter scarf</u> / <u>hat</u>.
                 f.

DRESS FOR THE SUN

Kimberly is wearing a <u>headwrap</u> / <u>straw hat</u>,
                g.

black <u>swimming trunks</u> / <u>swimsuit</u>, and a white
               h.

<u>cover-up</u> / <u>windbreaker</u>. Her <u>raincoat</u> / <u>umbrella</u>
  i.   **j.**

and <u>leggings</u> / <u>sunglasses</u> protect her from the sun.
       k.

3. **What about you? Circle the words to complete the sentences.**

    a. I <u>am</u> / <u>am not</u> wearing a jacket or coat today.

    b. I <u>wear</u> / <u>don't wear</u> sunglasses.

    c. I <u>sometimes</u> / <u>never</u> wear a hat.

See page 176 for listening practice.   **77**

Shoes and Accessories

A. **purchase**	1. suspenders	3. salesclerk	5. display case
B. **wait** in line	2. purses / handbags	4. customer	6. belts

13. wallet	17. shoulder bag	21. sole
14. change purse / coin purse	18. backpack	22. heel
15. cell phone holder	19. tote bag	23. toe
16. (wrist)watch	20. belt buckle	24. shoelaces

More vocabulary

gift: something you give or receive from friends or family for a special occasion

present: a gift

Grammar Point: object pronouns

My *sister* loves jewelry. I'll buy **her** a necklace.
My *dad* likes belts. I'll buy **him** a belt buckle.
My *friends* love scarves. I'll buy **them** scarves.

7. shoe department	9. bracelets	11. hats	C. **try on** shoes
8. jewelry department	10. necklaces	12. scarves	D. **assist** a customer

25. high heels	29. oxfords	33. chain	37. clip-on earrings
26. pumps	30. loafers	34. beads	38. pin
27. flats	31. hiking boots	35. locket	39. string of pearls
28. boots	32. tennis shoes	36. pierced earrings	40. ring

Ways to talk about accessories

I need <u>a hat</u> to wear with <u>this scarf</u>.
I'd like <u>earrings</u> to go with <u>the necklace</u>.
Do you have <u>a belt</u> that would go with my <u>shoes</u>?

Role play. Talk to a salesperson.

A: *Do you have <u>boots</u> that would go with <u>this skirt</u>?*
B: *Let me see. How about <u>these brown ones</u>?*
A: *Perfect. I also need…*

79

1. **Look at the top picture at pages 78–79. How many . . . can you see?**

a. salesclerks   3   **d.** customers trying on shoes   ____

b. customers waiting in line   ____   **e.** customers purchasing jewelry   ____

c. hats   ____   **f.** display cases   ____

2. **Look at the pictures. Label the items. Use the words in the box.**

backpack	bracelet	pin	change purse	earrings	~~wallet~~
locket	cell phone holder	ring	shoulder bag	tote bag	watch

a. _____wallet_____   **b.** _____   **c.** _____   **d.** _____

e. _____   **f.** _____   **g.** _____   **h.** _____

i. _____   **j.** _____   **k.** _____   **l.** _____

3. **Look at the answers in Exercise 2. Put the words in the correct columns.**

Jewelry Department		Other Accessories	
_____	_____	_____wallet_____	_____
_____	_____	_____	_____
_____	_____	_____	_____

4. Cross out the word that doesn't belong.

a. Things you wear around your neck   necklace   ~~belt~~   scarf   locket

b. Types of necklaces   beads   buckles   chain   string of pearls

c. Things you keep a change purse in   backpack   handbag   wallet   tote bag

d. Types of shoes   oxfords   boots   pumps   shoelaces

e. Parts of a shoe   sole   suspenders   heel   toe

5. Complete the ad. Use the words in the box.

~~pumps~~   flats   boots   hiking boots   loafers   oxfords   tennis shoes   high heels

SALE

The Good Sole

Save 20% on men's and women's shoes!

a. _pumps_

b. _____

c. _____

d. _____

e. _____

f. _____

g. _____

h. _____

Located at the Lincoln Mall.
Route 65

6. What about you? Check (✓) the items you have.

☐ chain   ☐ watch   ☐ pierced earrings

☐ clip-on earrings   ☐ belt buckle   ☐ cell phone holder

See page 176 for listening practice.

Describing Clothes

Sizes

1. extra small
2. small
3. medium
4. large
5. extra large
6. one-size-fits-all

Styles

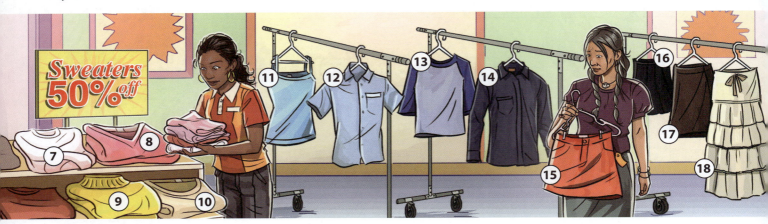

7. **crewneck** sweater

8. **V-neck** sweater

9. **turtleneck** sweater

10. **scoop neck** sweater

11. **sleeveless** shirt

12. **short-sleeved** shirt

13. **3/4-sleeved** shirt

14. **long-sleeved** shirt

15. **mini-**skirt

16. **short** skirt

17. **mid-length / calf-length** skirt

18. **long** skirt

Patterns

19. solid

20. striped

21. polka-dotted

22. plaid

23. print

24. checked

25. floral

26. paisley

Ask your classmates. Share the answers.

1. Do you prefer crewneck or V-neck sweaters?
2. Do you prefer checked or striped shirts?
3. Do you prefer short-sleeved or sleeveless shirts?

Role play. Talk to a salesperson.

A: *Excuse me. I'm looking for this V-neck sweater in large.*
B: *Here's a large. It's on sale for $19.99.*
A: *Wonderful! I'll take it. I'm also looking for…*

Comparing Clothing

27. **heavy** jacket	29. **tight** pants	31. **low** heels	33. **plain** blouse	35. **narrow** tie
28. **light** jacket	30. **loose** / **baggy** pants	32. **high** heels	34. **fancy** blouse	36. **wide** tie

Clothing Problems

37. It's **too small**.

38. It's **too big**.

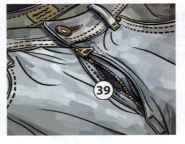

39. The zipper is **broken**.

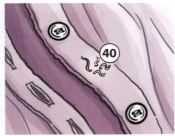

40. A button is **missing**.

41. It's **ripped** / **torn**.

42. It's **stained**.

43. It's **unraveling**.

44. It's **too expensive**.

More vocabulary

refund: money you get back when you return an item to the store
complaint: a statement that something is not right
customer service: the place customers go with their complaints

Role play. Return an item to a salesperson.

A: *Welcome to Shopmart. How may I help you?*
B: *This sweater is new, but it's unraveling.*
A: *I'm sorry. Would you like a refund?*

Describing Clothes

1. **Look at the T-shirts at page 82. *True* or *False*?**

    a. They come in six sizes. _____true_____   d. They are short-sleeved. _____

    b. They have a V-neck. _____   e. They are checked. _____

    c. They are solid blue. _____   f. They are stained. _____

2. **Look at pages 82–83. Match the opposites.**

    _5_ **a.** big   **1.** plain

    ___ **b.** fancy   **2.** wide

    ___ **c.** heavy   **3.** long

    ___ **d.** loose   **4.** tight

    ___ **e.** narrow   **5.** small

    ___ **f.** high   **6.** print

    ___ **g.** short   **7.** low

    ___ **h.** solid   **8.** light

3. **Look at the picture. Describe the problems.**

    a. His jeans are too _____baggy_____ and too _____.

    b. His sweater is too _____ and the sleeves are _____.

    c. His jacket sleeve is _____ and a button _____.

4. **Look at the order form. Circle the words to complete the statements.**

ITEM #	PAGE #	DESCRIPTION	SIZE	COLOR	QUANTITY	ITEM PRICE	TOTAL
563218	3	CREWNECK SWEATER	S	RED AND BLACK STRIPED	3	$15.00	$45.00
962143	12	JACKET	M	BLACK	1	$62.00	$62.00
583614	8	3/4-SLEEVED SHIRT	L	PAISLEY	1	$18.00	$18.00
769304	15	MINI-SKIRT	S	RED	1	$50.00	$50.00
216983	10	LOOSE JEANS	8	DARK BLUE	1	$98.00	$98.00

a. The customer wants extra-small / small crewneck sweaters.

b. She's ordering a long / large paisley shirt.

c. It's a 3/4-sleeved / sleeveless shirt.

d. She also wants a plaid / medium jacket.

e. The skirt is short / long.

f. The jeans are expensive / tight.

5. **What about you? Look at the ad. Choose two items to order. Add them to the order form in Exercise 4.**

men's and women's
turtlenecks
XS, S, M, L
100% cotton
308965.........$18.00

42

6. **What about you? Describe a problem you have or had with your clothes.**

Example: *My jacket zipper is broken.*

_____

See page 177 for listening practice.

Types of Material

1. cotton

2. linen

3. wool

4. cashmere

5. silk

6. leather

A Garment Factory

Parts of a Sewing Machine

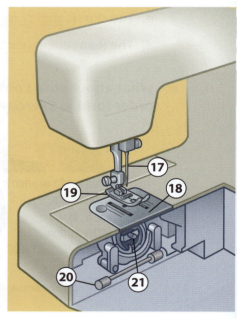

A. **sew** by machine

B. **sew** by hand

13. sewing machine

14. sewing machine operator

15. bolt of fabric

16. rack

17. needle

18. needle plate

19. presser foot

20. feed dog / feed bar

21. bobbin

More vocabulary
fashion designer: a person who makes original clothes
natural materials: cloth made from things that grow in nature
synthetic materials: cloth made by people, such as nylon

Use the new words.
Look at pages 86–87. Name the materials you see.

A: *That's <u>denim</u>.*
B: *That's <u>leather</u>.*

Types of Material

7. denim

8. suede

9. lace

10. velvet

11. corduroy

12. nylon

A Fabric Store

Closures

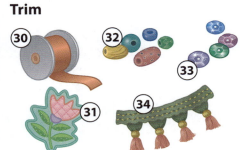

Trim

22. pattern
23. thread
24. button

25. zipper
26. snap
27. hook and eye

28. buckle
29. hook and loop fastener
30. ribbon

31. appliqué
32. beads

33. sequins
34. fringe

Making Clothes

1. **Look at the garment factory at page 86. How many . . . are there?**

   a. women sewing by hand   *1*

   b. women sewing by machine   ____

   c. bolts of fabric   ____

   d. shirts on the rack   ____

   e. sewing machine needles   ____

2. **Write the name of the material. Use the words in the box.**

cotton	~~cashmere~~	leather	linen	silk	wool

   a. _____*cashmere*_____    b.  _____   c. _____

   d.  _____   e.  _____   f. _____

3. **What about you? What materials are you wearing today? Write three sentences.**

   Example: *I'm wearing a cotton sweater.*

   _____

   _____

   _____

4. Look at pages 86–87. Cross out the word that doesn't belong.

a. Closures   zipper   snap   buckle   ~~ribbon~~

b. Trim   thread   sequins   fringe   beads

c. Material   cashmere   pattern   leather   nylon

d. Sewing machine parts   bobbin   rack   needle   feed dog

5. Look at the picture. Circle the words to complete the sentences.

Vilma is wearing a (denim) / wool jacket with buttons / snaps. Her jacket has beautiful
                          a.   **b.**

appliqués / sequins on it. Her husband, Enrique, is wearing a corduroy / suede jacket with
       c.   **d.**

fringe / ribbon. It's cold outside, but his jacket buckle / zipper is open. Their daughter,
   e.   **f.**

Rosa, is wearing a lace / velvet jacket with beads / thread. Her jacket is closed with
                  g.   **h.**

hooks and eyes / buttons.
     i.

6. What about you? What type of closures do your clothes have?

Example: *My shirt has buttons. My jeans have a zipper.*

See page 177 for listening practice.

Making Alterations

An Alterations Shop

1. dressmaker
2. dressmaker's dummy
3. tailor
4. collar
5. waistband
6. sleeve
7. pocket
8. hem
9. cuff

Sewing Supplies

10. needle
11. thread
12. (straight) pin
13. pin cushion
14. safety pin
15. thimble
16. pair of scissors
17. tape measure
18. seam ripper

Alterations

A. **Lengthen** the pants.

B. **Shorten** the pants.

C. **Let out** the pants.

D. **Take in** the pants.

Pair practice. Make new conversations.

A: *Would you hand me <u>the thread</u>?*
B: *OK. What are you going to do?*
A: *I'm going to <u>take in</u> these <u>pants</u>.*

Ask your classmates. Share the answers.

1. Is there an alterations shop near your home?
2. Do you ever go to a tailor or a dressmaker?
3. What sewing supplies do you have at home?

1. Look at page 90. Who is . . . ? Check (✓) the answers.

	Dressmaker	Tailor
a. working in the alterations shop	✓	✓
b. working on a dress	☐	☐
c. using a sewing machine	☐	☐
d. using a dummy	☐	☐
e. using a tape measure	☐	☐
f. using thread	☐	☐

2. Look at the pictures. Check (✓) the alterations the tailor made.

ALTERED STATES
TAILORS SINCE 1945

☑ repair zipper
☐ lengthen hem
☐ shorten hem
☐ take in waistband
☐ let out waistband
☐ repair pocket
☐ repair cuff
☐ repair collar

Before

After

3. List the items in the sewing basket.

_____tape measure_____   _____

_____   _____

_____   _____

_____   _____

_____

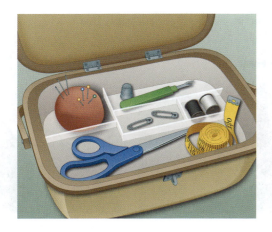

See page 178 for listening practice.

Describing Hair

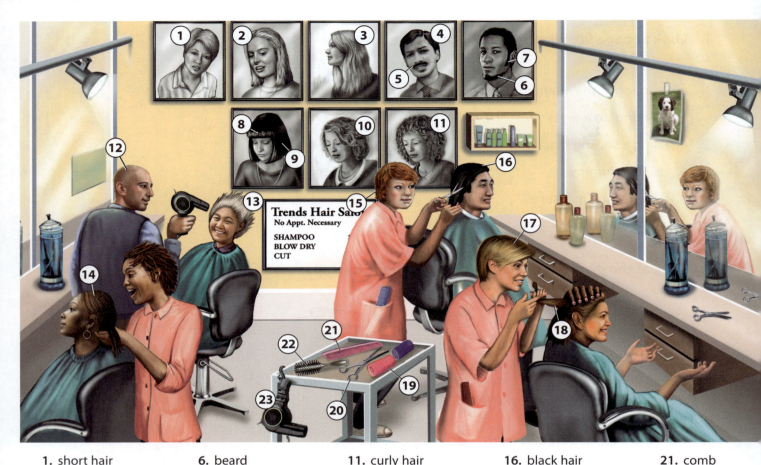

1. short hair
2. shoulder-length hair
3. long hair
4. part
5. mustache

6. beard
7. sideburns
8. bangs
9. straight hair
10. wavy hair

11. curly hair
12. bald
13. gray hair
14. corn rows
15. red hair

16. black hair
17. blond hair
18. brown hair
19. rollers
20. scissors

21. comb
22. brush
23. blow dryer

Style Hair

A. **cut** hair

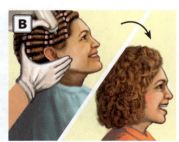

B. **perm** hair

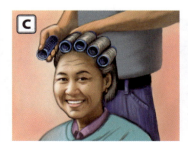

C. **set** hair

D. **color** hair / **dye** hair

Ways to talk about hair
Describe hair in this order: length, style, and then color.
She has <u>long</u>, <u>straight</u>, <u>brown</u> hair.

Role play. Talk to a stylist.
A: *I need a new hairstyle.*
B: *How about <u>short</u> and <u>straight</u>?*
A: *Great. Do you think I should <u>dye</u> it?*

1. Look at the top picture at page 92. How many . . . do you see?

a. combs ___5___   c. blow dryers ___   e. people with gray hair ___

b. rollers ___   d. brushes ___   f. scissors ___

2. Look at the pictures of Cindi. Check (✓) the things The Hair Salon did to Cindi's hair.

 Before

 Now

THE HAIR SALON

- ✓ cut
- ☐ set
- ☐ color
- ☐ perm

3. Circle the words to complete the paragraph about Cindi.

Cindi is very happy with her new hairstyle. Before, she had short / (long) curly / straight,
                                                        a.   b.

blond / brown hair with corn rows / bangs and a part / no part. Now she has very
        c.   d.   e.

long / short, curly / straight, red / black hair. Cindi looks great!
    f.   g.   h.

4. What about you? Draw a picture of a friend's hair. Check (✓) the correct boxes.
My friend has . . . .

☐ short hair   ☐ shoulder-length hair   ☐ long hair

☐ no hair (bald)   ☐ straight hair   ☐ wavy hair

☐ curly hair   ☐ a part   ☐ bangs

☐ corn rows   ☐ a mustache   ☐ a beard

☐ sideburns   ☐ _____ hair
                                     (list hair color)

See page 178 for listening practice.

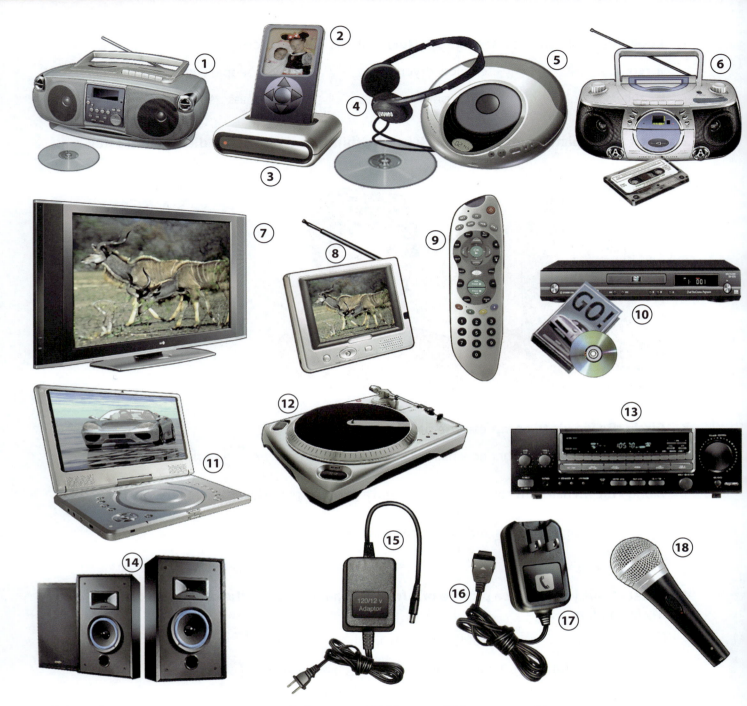

1. CD boombox

2. MP3 player

3. dock

4. headphones

5. personal CD player

6. portable cassette player

7. flat screen TV / flat panel TV

8. portable TV

9. universal remote

10. DVD player

11. portable DVD player

12. turntable

13. tuner

14. speakers

15. adapter

16. plug

17. charger

18. microphone

19. digital camera

20. memory card

21. film camera / 35 mm camera

22. film

23. zoom lens

24. camcorder

25. tripod

26. battery pack

27. battery charger

28. camera case

29. LCD projector

30. screen

31. photo album

32. digital photo album

33. out of focus

34. overexposed

35. underexposed

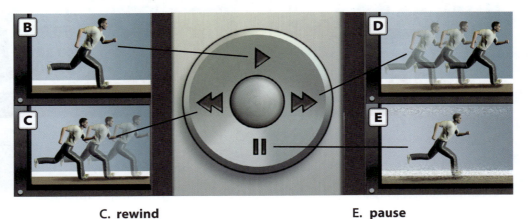

A. record

B. play

C. rewind

D. fast forward

E. pause

1. **Look at pages 94–95. Cross out the word that doesn't belong.**

a.	**Things you carry**	CD boombox	~~DVD player~~	portable cassette player
b.	**Things you watch**	flat screen TV	portable DVD player	microphone
c.	**Things that are small**	MP3 player	portable TV	tuner
d.	**Things for music**	adapter	speakers	turntable
e.	**Things that take pictures**	digital camera	LCD projector	film camera
f.	**Things for a camera**	dock	tripod	zoom lens

2. **Look at the ad. How much money can you save?**

a.	speakers	$25.00	**e.**	CD boombox	_____
b.	portable cassette player	_____	**f.**	MP3 player	_____
c.	personal CD player	_____	**g.**	35 mm camera	_____
d.	camcorder	_____	**h.**	digital camera	_____

3. Look at the universal remote buttons. Write the function. Use the words in the box.

fast forward	pause	play	~~rewind~~

a. _____rewind_____   b. _____   c. _____   d. _____

4. Look at the pictures. Which one is . . . ? Write the number.

1.    2.    3.

4.    5.

a. overexposed __3__   d. from black and white film ____

b. good for a photo album ____   e. underexposed ____

c. out of focus ____

5. What about you? Check (✓) the items you have. Circle the items you want.

☐ CD boombox   ☐ portable DVD palyer   ☐ tripod

☐ MP3 player   ☐ digital camera   ☐ camera case

☐ personal CD player   ☐ film camera   ☐ LCD projector

☐ flat screen TV   ☐ camcorder   ☐ photo album

See page 179 for listening practice.

Medical Specialists

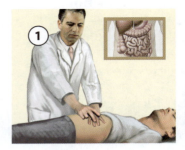

1. internist

2. obstetrician

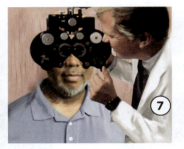

3. cardiologist

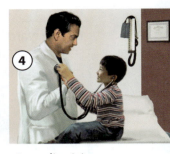

4. pediatrician

5. oncologist

6. radiologist

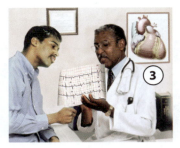

7. ophthalmologist

8. psychiatrist

Nursing Staff

9. surgical nurse

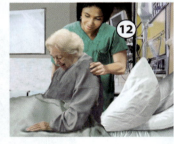

10. registered nurse (RN)

11. licensed practical nurse (LPN)

12. certified nursing assistant (CNA)

Hospital Staff

13. administrator

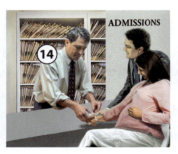

14. admissions clerk

15. dietician

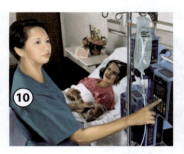

16. orderly

More vocabulary

Gynecologists examine and treat women.
Nurse practitioners can give medical exams.
Nurse midwives deliver babies.

Chiropractors move the spine to improve health.
Orthopedists treat bone and joint problems.

A Hospital Room

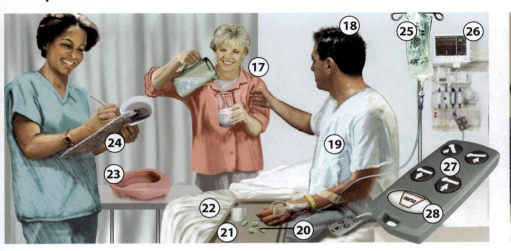

17. volunteer	**21.** bed table	**25.** IV (intravenous drip)
18. patient	**22.** hospital bed	**26.** vital signs monitor
19. hospital gown	**23.** bed pan	**27.** bed control
20. medication	**24.** medical chart	**28.** call button

Lab

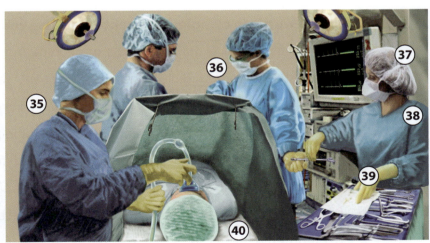

29. phlebotomist

30. blood work / blood test

31. medical waste disposal

Emergency Room Entrance

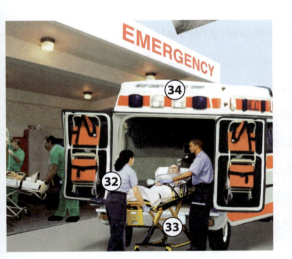

32. emergency medical technician (EMT)

33. stretcher / gurney

34. ambulance

Operating Room

35. anesthesiologist	**37.** surgical cap	**39.** surgical gloves
36. surgeon	**38.** surgical gown	**40.** operating table

Dictate to your partner. Take turns.

A: *Write this sentence.* <u>*She's a volunteer.*</u>
B: <u>*She's a*</u> *what?*
A: <u>*Volunteer.*</u> *That's* <u>*v-o-l-u-n-t-e-e-r.*</u>

Role play. Ask about a doctor.

A: *I need to find a good* <u>*surgeon*</u>.
B: <u>*Dr. Jones*</u> *is a great* <u>*surgeon*</u>. *You should call* <u>*him*</u>.
A: *I will! Please give me* <u>*his*</u> *number.*

The Hospital

1. Look at pages 98–99. Match.

<u> 5 </u> **a.** general health problems

____ **b.** heart

____ **c.** cancer

____ **d.** depression

____ **e.** eyes

____ **f.** children

____ **g.** pregnant women

____ **h.** x-rays

1. radiologist

2. oncologist

3. ophthalmologist

4. psychiatrist

5. internist

6. pediatrician

7. cardiologist

8. obstetrician

2. Circle the words to complete the sentences. Use your dictionary for help.

  a. The internist / <u>surgical nurse</u> helps the surgeon during an operation.

  b. The <u>anesthesiologist / radiologist</u> makes the patient "sleep" on the operating table.

  c. The <u>emergency medical technician / pediatrician</u> takes the patient out of the ambulance.

  d. The <u>oncologist / phlebotomist</u> takes the patient's blood for blood tests.

  e. The <u>admissions clerk / volunteer</u> works in the hospital for no pay.

  f. The <u>certified nursing assistant / dietician</u> plans the patient's food.

  g. The <u>administrator / orderly</u> takes the patient from place to place.

  h. The <u>registered nurse / surgical nurse</u> checks the patient's IV.

  i. The <u>licensed practical nurse / phlebotomist</u> takes the patient's blood pressure.

3. Write the full forms. Use your dictionary for help.

  a. IV   <u>   *intravenous drip*   </u>   **d.** LPN   <u>   </u>

  b. EMT <u>   </u>   **e.** RN   <u>   </u>

  c. CNA <u>   </u>

4. **Look at the hospital room at page 99.** *True* **or** *False*?

a. The patient is on a stretcher. _____false_____

b. There's a bed pan near the bed. _____

c. The volunteer is carrying medication. _____

d. The nurse is wearing a hospital gown. _____

e. There's medication on the bed table. _____

f. The vital signs monitor is near the hospital bed. _____

g. The patient is using the call button now. _____

5. **Look at the picture and the supply list. Match.**

Supplies

a. __3__ intravenous drip

b. _____ surgical gloves

c. _____ medical charts

d. _____ medical waste disposal

e. _____ surgical caps

f. _____ surgical gowns

See page 179 for listening practice.

Inside and Outside the Body

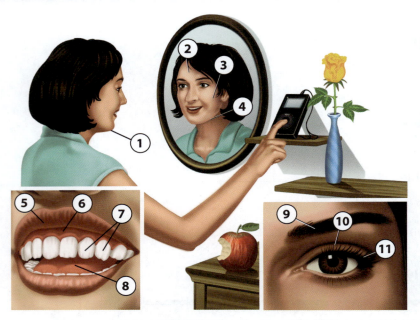

The Face

1. chin
2. forehead
3. cheek
4. jaw

The Mouth

5. lip
6. gums
7. teeth
8. tongue

The Eye

9. eyebrow
10. eyelid
11. eyelashes

The Senses

A. **see**
B. **hear**
C. **smell**
D. **taste**
E. **touch**

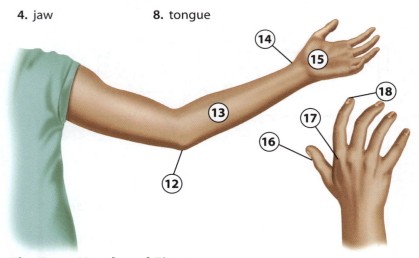

The Arm, Hand, and Fingers

12. elbow
13. forearm
14. wrist
15. palm
16. thumb
17. knuckle
18. fingernail

The Leg and Foot

19. thigh
20. knee
21. shin
22. calf
23. ankle
24. heel

More vocabulary

torso: the part of the body from the shoulders to the pelvis
limbs: arms and legs
toenail: the nail on your toe

Pair practice. Make new conversations.

A: *Is your arm OK?*
B: *Yes, but now my elbow hurts.*
A: *I'm sorry to hear that.*

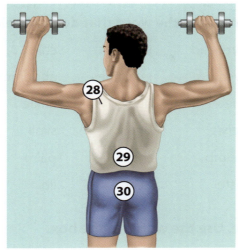

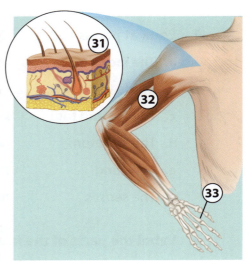

25. chest

26. breast

27. abdomen

28. shoulder blade

29. lower back

30. buttocks

31. skin

32. muscle

33. bone

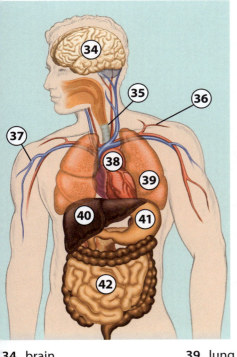

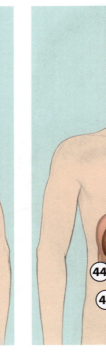

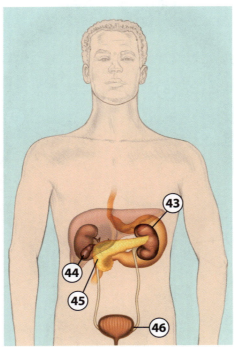

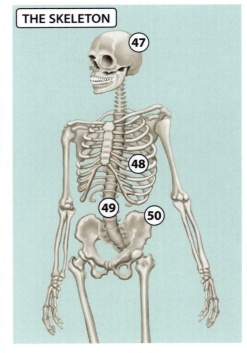

THE SKELETON

34. brain

35. throat

36. artery

37. vein

38. heart

39. lung

40. liver

41. stomach

42. intestines

43. kidney

44. gallbladder

45. pancreas

46. bladder

47. skull

48. rib cage

49. spinal column

50. pelvis

103

1. Look at pages 102–103. Cross out the word that doesn't belong.

a. The face	forehead	jaw	chin	~~toe~~
b. Inside the body	liver	intestines	abdomen	stomach
c. The leg and foot	knee	heel	ankle	tongue
d. The skeleton	pelvis	brain	skull	rib cage
e. The hand	thumb	shin	palm	wrist
f. The senses	taste	hear	lip	smell

2. Label the parts of the face. Use the words in the box.

eyebrow	eyelashes	eyelid	cheek	chin
~~forehead~~	jaw	lip	teeth	

a. _forehead_

b. _____

c. _____

d. _____

e. _____

f. _____

g. _____

h. _____

i. _____

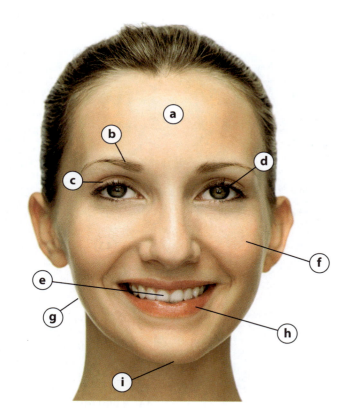

3. **Look at the picture. Check (✓) the parts of the body that are NOT covered by clothes.**

- [✓] arms
- [ ] calves
- [ ] elbows
- [ ] feet
- [ ] hands
- [ ] knees
- [ ] lower back
- [ ] shoulder blades
- [ ] buttocks
- [ ] chest
- [ ] fingers
- [ ] forearms
- [ ] head
- [ ] legs
- [ ] shins
- [ ] jaw

4. **Match.**

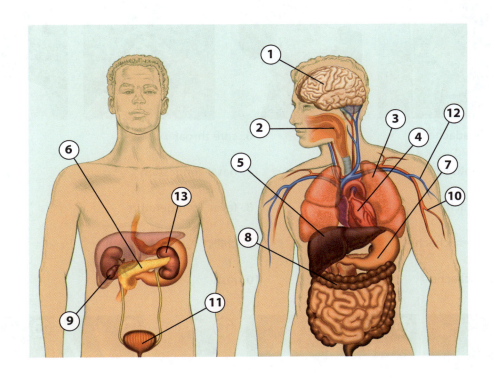

- __4__ a. heart
- ____ b. kidney
- ____ c. lung
- ____ d. liver
- ____ e. gallbladder
- ____ f. bladder
- ____ g. throat
- ____ h. stomach
- ____ i. pancreas
- ____ j. brain
- ____ k. intestines
- ____ l. artery
- ____ m. vein

5. **What about you? <u>Underline</u> the words for parts of the body that are NOT OK for men to show on the street in your native country. Circle the words for parts of the body that are NOT OK for women to show.**

arms	abdomen	elbows	face	mouth
ankles	chest	knees	calves	feet

See page 179 for listening practice.

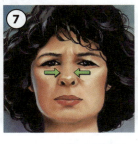
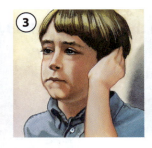

1. headache
2. toothache
3. earache
4. stomachache
5. backache

6. sore throat
7. nasal congestion
8. fever / temperature
9. chills
10. rash

A. **cough**
B. **sneeze**
C. **feel** dizzy
D. **feel** nauseous
E. **throw up / vomit**

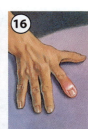

11. insect bite
12. bruise
13. cut
14. sunburn
15. blister
16. swollen finger
17. bloody nose
18. sprained ankle

Look at the pictures.
Describe the symptoms and injuries.

A: *He has a backache.*
B: *She has a toothache.*

Think about it. Discuss.
1. What are some common cold symptoms?
2. What do you recommend for a stomachache?
3. What is the best way to stop a bloody nose?

1. **Look at page 106. *True* or *False*?**

    a. The man in picture 11 has an insect bite on his right arm.   _____true_____

    b. The man in picture 13 has a cut on his thumb.   _____

    c. The man in picture 15 has a blister on his hand.   _____

    d. The woman in picture 16 has a swollen toe.   _____

    e. The woman in picture 18 has a sprained ankle.   _____

2. **Look at Tania's medicine. Complete the form. Look at page 106 for help.**

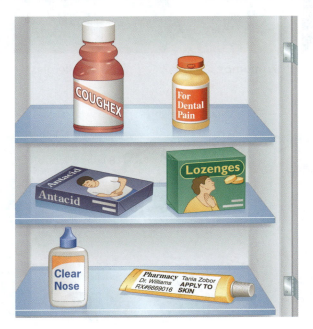

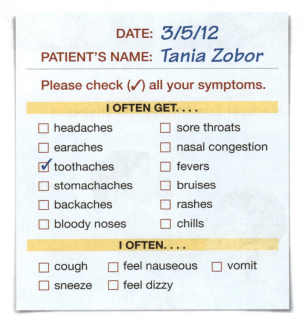

DATE: **3/5/12**

PATIENT'S NAME: **Tania Zobor**

Please check (✓) all your symptoms.

I OFTEN GET. . . .	
☐ headaches	☐ sore throats
☐ earaches	☐ nasal congestion
✓ toothaches	☐ fevers
☐ stomachaches	☐ bruises
☐ backaches	☐ rashes
☐ bloody noses	☐ chills

I OFTEN. . . .		
☐ cough	☐ feel nauseous	☐ vomit
☐ sneeze	☐ feel dizzy	

3. **What about you? Complete the form. Use your own information or information about someone you know.**

PATIENT'S NAME: _____

Please check (✓) all your symptoms.

I OFTEN GET. . . .		
☐ headaches	☐ backaches	☐ fevers
☐ earaches	☐ bloody noses	☐ bruises
☐ toothaches	☐ sore throats	☐ rashes
☐ stomachaches	☐ nasal congestion	☐ chills

I OFTEN. . . .	
☐ cough	☐ feel dizzy
☐ sneeze	☐ vomit
☐ feel nauseous	

See page 180 for listening practice.

Illnesses and Medical Conditions

Common Illnesses and Childhood Diseases

1. cold

2. flu

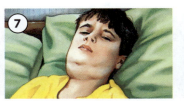

3. ear infection

4. strep throat

5. measles

6. chicken pox

7. mumps

8. allergies

Serious Medical Conditions and Diseases

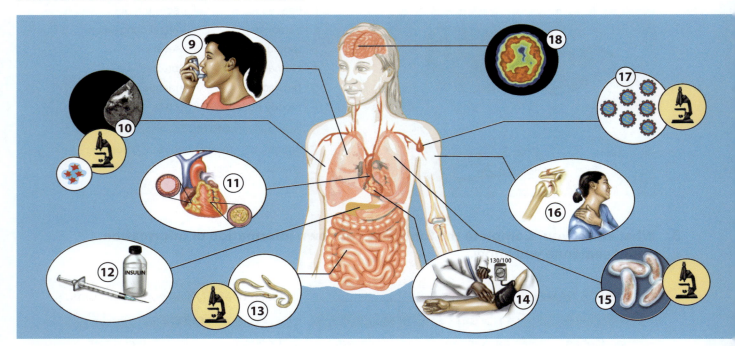

9. asthma

10. cancer

11. heart disease

12. diabetes

13. intestinal parasites

14. high blood pressure / hypertension

15. TB (tuberculosis)

16. arthritis

17. HIV (human immunodeficiency virus)

18. dementia

More vocabulary

AIDS (acquired immune deficiency syndrome): a medical condition that results from contracting the HIV virus

Alzheimer's disease: a disease that causes dementia

coronary disease: heart disease

infectious disease: a disease that is spread through air or water

influenza: flu

1. **Look at the bottom picture at page 108. Write the illness or medical condition.**

   a. lungs _____*TB*_____ and _____

   b. heart and arteries _____ and _____

   c. pancreas _____

   d. brain _____

   e. blood _____

   f. joints _____

2. **Look at the photos of Mehmet when he was a child. Complete the form.**

  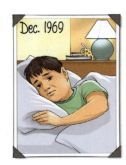 

EDG EARLY DIAGNOSIS CENTER	NAME: *Mehmet Caner*	DATE OF BIRTH: *April 18, 1959*
CHECK (✓) THE ILLNESSES OR CONDITIONS YOU HAD AS A CHILD.		
☐ DIABETES	☐ CHICKEN POX	☐ MUMPS
☐ INTESTINAL PARASITES	☐ ASTHMA	☐ ALLERGIES
☑ EAR INFECTIONS	☐ STREP THROAT	

3. **What about you? Complete the form. Use your own information or information about someone you know.**

EDG EARLY DIAGNOSIS CENTER	NAME:	DATE OF BIRTH:
CHECK (✓) THE ILLNESSES OR CONDITIONS YOU HAD AS A CHILD.		
☐ DIABETES	☐ CHICKEN POX	☐ MUMPS
☐ INTESTINAL PARASITES	☐ ASTHMA	☐ ALLERGIES
☐ EAR INFECTIONS	☐ STREP THROAT	

See page 180 for listening practice.

Medical Emergencies

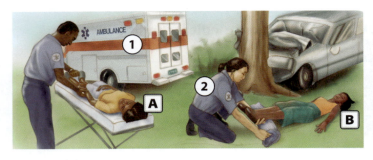  

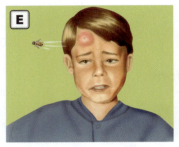  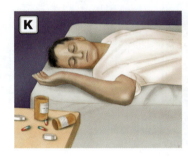 

  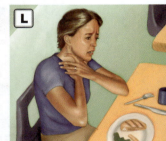

   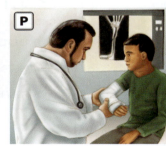

1. ambulance

2. paramedic

A. **be** unconscious

B. **be** in shock

C. **be** injured / **be** hurt

D. **have** a heart attack

E. **have** an allergic reaction

F. **get** an electric shock

G. **get** frostbite

H. **burn** (your)self

I. **drown**

J. **swallow** poison

K. **overdose** on drugs

L. **choke**

M. **bleed**

N. **can't breathe**

O. **fall**

P. **break** a bone

Grammar Point: past tense

For past tense add –ed:
burned, drowned, swallowed, overdosed, choked

These verbs are different (irregular):

be – was, were	bleed – bled	fall – fell
have – had	can't – couldn't	
get – got	break – broke	

1. **Look at page 110. *True* or *False*?**

   a. A paramedic is helping an unconscious woman. _____*true*_____

   b. The woman in the red sweater is in shock. _____

   c. The man near the bookcase is hurt. _____

   d. The boy in the dark blue shirt is having an allergic reaction. _____

   e. The child in the swimming pool is getting frostbite. _____

   f. The woman at the table is choking. _____

   g. The boy in the doctor's office broke a leg. _____

   h. The man holding his chest is having a heart attack. _____

2. **Look at the chart. How did the people injure themselves? Circle the words.**

Number of Injuries in the United States in a Year		
Product	**Estimated Injuries**	**People probably . . . .**
a. Stairs	2,074,047	had an allergic reaction / (fell)
b. Bikes	535,100	overdosed / fell
c. Bathtubs / Showers	304,880	broke bones / got frostbite
d. TVs	53,471	were in shock / got an electric shock
e. Razors	36,612	bled / couldn't breathe
f. Stoves / Ovens	43,356	burned themselves / choked
g. Irons	12,818	drowned / burned themselves

Based on information from: *Consumer Product Safety Review,*
2003. www.cpsc.gov.

3. **What about you? Check (✓) the emergencies that have happened to you. When or where did they happen?**

   Emergency **When or Where**

   ☐ I had an allergic reaction to _____. _____

   ☐ I fell. _____

   ☐ I broke my _____. _____

   ☐ Other: _____. _____

See page 180 for listening practice. **111**

First Aid

First Aid

1. first aid kit

2. first aid manual

3. medical emergency bracelet

Inside the Kit

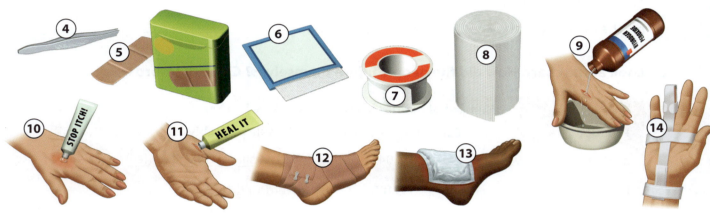

4. tweezers

5. adhesive bandage

6. sterile pad

7. sterile tape

8. gauze

9. hydrogen peroxide

10. antihistamine cream

11. antibacterial ointment

12. elastic bandage

13. ice pack

14. splint

First Aid Procedures

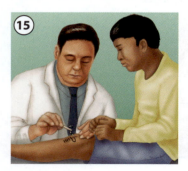 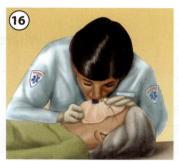 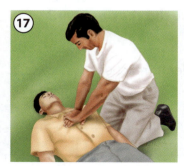 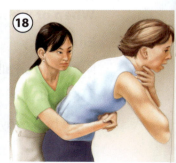

15. stitches

16. rescue breathing

17. CPR (cardiopulmonary resuscitation)

18. Heimlich maneuver

Pair practice. Make new conversations.

A: *What do we need in the first aid kit?*
B: *We need <u>tweezers</u> and <u>gauze</u>.*
A: *I think we need <u>sterile tape</u>, too.*

Think about it. Discuss.

1. What are the three most important first aid items? Why?
2. Which first aid procedures should everyone know? Why?
3. What are some good places to keep a first aid kit?

1. Look at page 112. Write the first aid item for these conditions.

a. rash on hand _antihistamine cream_

b. broken finger _____

c. swollen foot _____ or _____

d. infected cut _____ or _____

2. Look at Chen's first aid kit. Check (✓) the items he has.

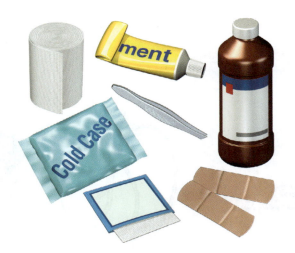

FAMILY FIRST AID AND EMERGENCY PREPAREDNESS

✓ adhesive bandages	☐ first aid manual
☐ antihistamine cream	☐ antibacterial ointment
☐ elastic bandage	☐ hydrogen peroxide
☐ splint	☐ ice pack
☐ sterile pad	☐ sterile tape
☐ gauze	☐ tweezers

3. What about you? Check (✓) the first aid items you have at home. Then, check (✓) the things you can do.

At home I have	
☐ adhesive bandages	☐ first aid manual
☐ antihistamine cream	☐ antibacterial ointment
☐ elastic bandages	☐ hydrogen peroxide
☐ splints	☐ ice packs
☐ sterile pads	☐ sterile tape
☐ gauze	☐ tweezers

I can do . . . .
☐ CPR
☐ rescue breathing
☐ the Heimlich maneuver

See page 181 for listening practice.

Medical Care

In the Waiting Room

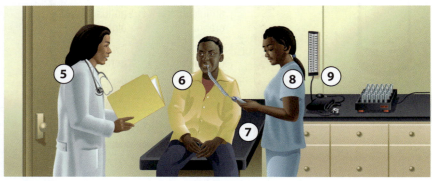

3 HEALTH FIRST

Name: Andre Zolmar
Group Number: 98765
Membership Number: 60756789

4 Health Form

Name: Andre Zolmar
Date of birth: July 8, 1973
Current symptoms: stomachache

Health History:

Childhood Diseases:
☑ chicken pox
☑ diphtheria
☑ rubella
☑ measles
☐ mumps
☐ other

Description of symptoms:

1. appointment
2. receptionist
3. health insurance card
4. health history form

In the Examining Room

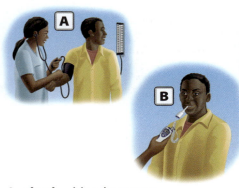

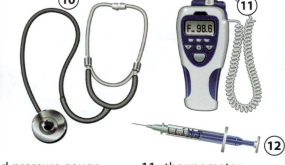

5. doctor
6. patient
7. examination table
8. nurse
9. blood pressure gauge
10. stethoscope
11. thermometer
12. syringe

Medical Procedures

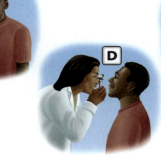

A. **check**…blood pressure

B. **take**…temperature

C. **listen** to…heart

D. **examine**…eyes

E. **examine**…throat

F. **draw**…blood

Grammar Point: future tense with *will* + verb

To show a future action, use *will* + verb.
The subject pronoun contraction of *will* is -*'ll*.
She **will draw** your blood. = She**'ll draw** your blood.

Role play. Talk to a medical receptionist.

A: *Will the nurse _examine my eyes_?*
B: *No, but she'll _draw your blood_.*
A: *What will the doctor do?*

1. **Look at page 114. Who . . . ? Check (✓) the columns.**

	Patient	Receptionist	Doctor	Nurse
a. has an appointment	✓			
b. checks blood pressure				
c. has a thermometer				
d. examines the throat				
e. has a health insurance card				
f. is on the examination table				
g. is holding a health history form				
h. has a stethoscope				

2. **Look at the doctor's notes. Which medical instrument did the doctor use? Match.**

MEDICAL CENTER
Dr. D. Ngoc Huynh
DATE: 3/5/12

PATIENT'S NAME: Carla Vega

1. checked BP—120/80
2. took temp.—98.6°
3. listened to lungs—clear
4. gave flu immunization

__4__ **a.** syringe

____ **b.** thermometer

____ **c.** blood pressure gauge

____ **d.** stethoscope

3. **What about you? Think of the last time you saw the doctor. How long were you . . . ?**

in the waiting room _____

in the examining room _____

on the examination table _____

Did the doctor or nurse . . . ? Check (✓) the answers.

☐ check your blood pressure   ☐ draw blood

☐ examine your eyes   ☐ take your temperature

See page 181 for listening practice.

A Pharmacy

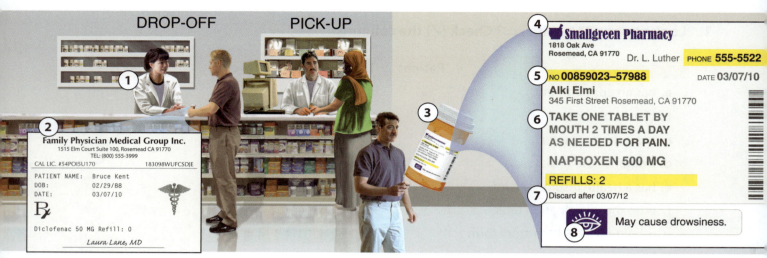

DROP-OFF PICK-UP

Smallgreen Pharmacy
1818 Oak Ave
Rosemead, CA 91770
Dr. L. Luther   PHONE **555-5522**

NO **00859023–57988**   DATE **03/07/10**

Alki Elmi
345 First Street Rosemead, CA 91770

TAKE ONE TABLET BY
MOUTH 2 TIMES A DAY
AS NEEDED FOR PAIN.

NAPROXEN 500 MG

REFILLS: 2

Discard after 03/07/12

👁 May cause drowsiness.

Family Physician Medical Group Inc.
1515 Elm Court Suite 100, Rosemead CA 91770
TEL: (800) 555-3999

CAL LIC. #54POI5U170   183098WUFCSDJE

PATIENT NAME: Bruce Kent
DOB: 02/29/88
DATE: 03/07/10

℞

Diclofenac 50 MG Refill: 0

Laura Lane, MD

1. pharmacist	3. prescription medication	5. prescription number	7. expiration date
2. prescription	4. prescription label	6. dosage	8. warning label

Medical Warnings

A. **Take** with food or milk.

B. **Take** one hour before eating.

C. **Finish** all medication.

D. **Do not take** with dairy products.

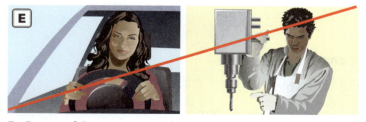

E. **Do not drive or operate** heavy machinery.

F. **Do not drink** alcohol.

More vocabulary

prescribe medication: to write a prescription
fill prescriptions: to prepare medication for patients
pick up a prescription: to get prescription medication

Role play. Talk to the pharmacist.

A: *Hi. I need to pick up a prescription for <u>Jones</u>.*
B: *Here's your medication, <u>Mr. Jones</u>. Take these <u>once a day with milk or food</u>.*

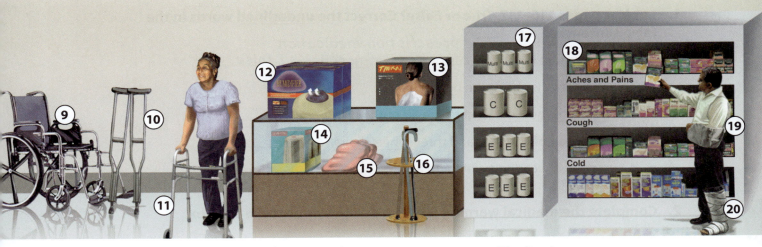

9. wheelchair	**13.** heating pad	**17.** vitamins
10. crutches	**14.** air purifier	**18.** over-the-counter medication
11. walker	**15.** hot water bottle	**19.** sling
12. humidifier	**16.** cane	**20.** cast

Types of Medication

21. pill	**22.** tablet	**23.** capsule	**24.** ointment	**25.** cream

Over-the-Counter Medication

26. pain reliever	**28.** antacid	**30.** throat lozenges	**32.** nasal spray
27. cold tablets	**29.** cough syrup	**31.** eye drops	**33.** inhaler

Ways to talk about medication

Use *take* for pills, tablets, capsules, and cough syrup.
Use *apply* for ointments and creams.
Use *use* for drops, nasal sprays, and inhalers.

Ask your classmates. Share the answers.

1. What pharmacy do you go to?
2. Do you ever ask the pharmacist for advice?
3. Do you take any vitamins? Which ones?

117

1. Look at pages 116–117. *True* or *False*? Correct the <u>underlined</u> words in the false sentences.

                        prescription medication

a. The pharmacist is giving a customer <u>a ~~prescription~~</u>.   <u> *false* </u>

b. The humidifier is above the <u>heating pad</u>.   _____

c. The <u>hot water bottle</u> is next to the air purifier.   _____

d. There is a pair of crutches and three <u>wheelchairs</u>.   _____

e. A customer is wearing a sling and <u>a cast</u>.   _____

2. Complete the medical warning labels. Use the sentences in the box.

> Take with dairy products.   Do not take with dairy products.   Finish all medication.
> ~~Do not drive or operate heavy machinery.~~   Take with food or milk.   Do not drink alcohol.

a.

Do not drive or operate heavy machinery.
when taking this medicine

b.

c.

d.

e.
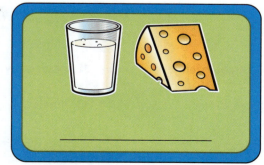

f.

when taking this medicine

3. Look at the picture. Circle the words to complete the sentences.

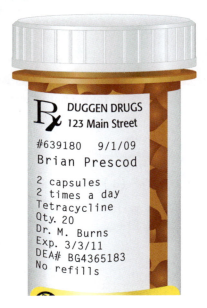

a. Brian got over-the-counter / (prescription) medication.

b. The name of the pharmacist / pharmacy is Duggen Drugs.

c. The bottle contains capsules / tablets.

d. The prescription number is 20 / 639180.

e. The prescription / warning label says, "Do not take with dairy products."

f. Brian can't drink water / eat cheese with this medicine.

g. The medicine isn't good after September 2009 / March 2011.

h. The dosage is two / four capsules every day.

4. What about you? Check (✓) the items you think are in your medicine cabinet. Then, check your answers at home.

☐ pain reliever

☐ cold tablets

☐ antacid

☐ cream

☐ cough syrup

☐ throat lozenges

☐ nasal spray

☐ ointment

☐ eye drops

☐ vitamins

See page 181 for listening practice.

Personal Hygiene

A. **take** a shower

B. **take** a bath / **bathe**

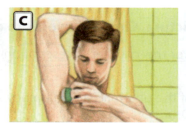

C. **use** deodorant

D. **put on** sunscreen

1. shower cap

2. shower gel

3. soap

4. bath powder

5. deodorant / antiperspirant

6. perfume / cologne

7. sunscreen

8. sunblock

9. body lotion / moisturizer

E. **wash**…hair

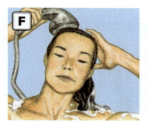

F. **rinse**…hair

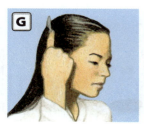

G. **comb**…hair

H. **dry**…hair

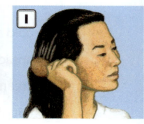

I. **brush**…hair

10. shampoo

11. conditioner

12. hair spray

13. comb

14. brush

15. pick

16. hair gel

17. curling iron

18. blow dryer

19. hair clip

20. barrette

21. bobby pins

More vocabulary

unscented: a product without perfume or scent
hypoallergenic: a product that is better for people
with allergies

Think about it. Discuss.

1. Which personal hygiene products should someone use
   before a job interview?
2. What is the right age to start wearing makeup? Why?

 **J. brush**…teeth

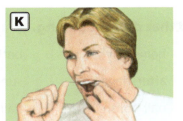 **K. floss**…teeth

 **L. gargle**

  **M. shave**

22. toothbrush

23. toothpaste

24. dental floss

25. mouthwash

26. electric shaver

27. razor

28. razorblade

29. shaving cream

30. aftershave

 **N. cut**…nails

 **O. polish**…nails

 **P. put on / apply**

 **Q. take off / remove**

 **Makeup**

31. nail clipper

32. emery board

33. nail polish

34. eyebrow pencil

35. eye shadow

36. eyeliner

37. blush

38. lipstick

39. mascara

40. foundation

41. face powder

42. makeup remover

Personal Hygiene

1. **Look at pages 120–121. Cross out the word that doesn't belong.**

   a. shower cap   soap   ~~hair spray~~   bath powder

   b. electric shaver   razorblades   aftershave   sunscreen

   c. hair clip   emery board   nail polish   nail clipper

   d. barrettes   eyebrow pencil   bobby pins   hair gel

   e. blush   foundation   eyeliner   deodorant

   f. body lotion   shampoo   blow dryer   conditioner

   g. toothbrush   comb   dental floss   toothpaste

2. **Look at Exercise 1. Write the letter of the items that you need for these activities.**

   _d_ 1. do your hair   ___ 5. shave

   ___ 2. take a shower   ___ 6. wash and dry your hair

   ___ 3. put on makeup   ___ 7. brush your teeth

   ___ 4. do your nails

3. **Look at the checklist. Check (✓) the items that Teresa packed.**

   Travel Packing List

   to pack for **San Diego**

☑ bath powder	☐ mouthwash
☐ blow dryer	☐ nail clipper
☐ bobby pins	☐ nail polish
☐ brush	☐ perfume
☐ comb	☐ razor
☐ conditioner	☐ shampoo
☐ curling iron	☐ shaving cream
☐ dental floss	☐ shower cap
☐ deodorant	☐ soap
☐ emery board	☐ sunscreen
☐ lipstick	☐ toothbrush
☐ mascara	☐ toothpaste

4. Teresa is at the hotel. Go back to the checklist in Exercise 3. Check (✓) the additional items that Teresa has now.

5. What does Teresa still need? Complete her shopping list.

HOTEL KENT

TO BUY

bobby pins

_____

_____

_____

_____

6. What about you? How often do you use . . . ? Check (✓) the columns.

	Every Day	Sometimes	Never
sunblock			
shower gel			
perfume or cologne			
hair spray			
dental floss			
body lotion or moisturizer			
mouthwash			
Other: _____			

See page 182 for listening practice.

Office Skills

Customers need better service…

Scan Complete

Let's meet at 2:00.

Sure.

Dear Mr. Smith…

Hello. ABC Company. How may I help you?

Please hold.

Mr. Perez, I'm transferring you.

Hello. This is Sue Jones. Please call me.

Message Pad
Call From: Ana Puerta
Tel: 555-1234
Message:
Please Call

This is Lee Tran. Please call me back.

Office Skills

A. **type** a letter

B. **enter** data

C. **transcribe** notes

D. **make** copies

E. **collate** papers

F. **staple**

G. **fax** a document

H. **scan** a document

I. **print** a document

J. **schedule** a meeting

K. **take** dictation

L. **organize** materials

Telephone Skills

M. **greet** the caller

N. **put** the caller on hold

O. **transfer** the call

P. **leave** a message

Q. **take** a message

R. **check** messages

124

1. Look at page 124. For which skills do the employees need . . . ?
Put the words in the correct columns.

A Computer	Paper	
type a letter	_type a letter_	_____
_____	_____	_____
_____	_____	_____
_____	_____	_____
	_____	

2. Match.

_2_ a.
> Smith, Cohen, and Soto.
> Good morning.

1. put the caller on hold

___ b.
> Give me your name and number,
> and he'll call you back.

2. greet the caller

___ c.
> I'll connect you to
> Ms. Soto's office.

3. transfer the call

___ d.
> One minute, please.
> I'll see if she's in her office.

4. take a message

3. What about you? Check (✓) the office skills you have.

☐ type a letter   ☐ collate papers

☐ enter data   ☐ staple

☐ transcribe notes   ☐ scan a document

☐ take dictation   ☐ fax a document

☐ organize materials   ☐ print a document

☐ make copies   ☐ take a message

See page 182 for listening practice.

1. supply cabinet
2. clerk
3. janitor
4. conference room
5. executive
6. presentation
7. cubicle
8. office manager
9. desk
10. file clerk
11. file cabinet
12. computer technician
13. PBX
14. receptionist
15. reception area
16. waiting area

Ways to greet a receptionist

I'm here for a _job interview_.
I have a _9:00 a.m._ appointment with _Mr. Lee_.
I'd like to leave a message _for Mr. Lee_.

Role play. Talk to a receptionist.

A: *Hello. How can I help you?*
B: *I'm here for a job interview with Mr. Lee.*
A: *OK. What is your name?*

Office Equipment

17. computer

18. inkjet printer

19. laser printer

20. scanner

21. fax machine

22. paper cutter

23. photocopier

24. paper shredder

25. calculator

26. electric pencil sharpener

27. postal scale

Office Supplies

28. stapler

29. staples

30. clear tape

31. paper clip

32. packing tape

33. glue

34. rubber band

35. pushpin

36. correction fluid

37. correction tape

38. legal pad

39. sticky notes

40. mailer

41. mailing label

42. letterhead / stationery

43. envelope

44. rotary card file

45. ink cartridge

46. ink pad

47. stamp

48. appointment book

49. organizer

50. file folder

1. **Look at pages 126–127. *True* or *False*? Correct the <u>underlined</u> words in the false sentences.**

   a. The receptionist is in the <u>conference room</u>.   *reception area* (written above, conference room crossed out)   _____*false*_____

   b. The office manager is at his desk in a <u>cubicle</u>.   _____

   c. The <u>clerk</u> is cleaning the floor.   _____

   d. The computer technician is working on a <u>scanner</u>.   _____

   e. The <u>executive</u> is at a presentation.   _____

   f. The <u>file clerk</u> is at the file cabinet.   _____

2. **Look at the pictures. What do the office workers need? Use the words in the box.**

calculator	electric pencil sharpener	file folder	mailing label	~~staples~~
paper cutter	photocopier	fax machine	postal scale	

a. _____*staples*_____

b. _____

c. _____

d. _____

e. _____

f. _____

g. _____

h. _____

i. _____

3. Look at the supply cabinet. Complete the office inventory.

1 <u>rotary card file</u>
6 bottles of _____
2 bottles of _____
1 box of _____
2 boxes of _____
3 boxes of _____
4 rolls of _____
5 rolls of _____
2 _____ pads
3 _____ pads
4 _____ pads
4 _____
2 _____
3 _____
1 bag of _____

4. What about you? How often do you use . . . ? Check (✓) the columns.

	Often	Sometimes	Never
a fax machine			
sticky notes			
an inkjet printer			
a laser printer			
an organizer			
an appointment book			
a rotary card file			
a paper shredder			

See page 182 for listening practice.

Computers

Desktop Computer

1. surge protector
2. power cord
3. tower
4. microprocessor / CPU
5. motherboard

6. hard drive
7. USB port
8. flash drive
9. DVD and CD-ROM drive
10. software

11. monitor /screen
12. webcam
13. cable
14. keyboard
15. mouse

16. laptop
17. printer

Keyboarding

A. **type**

B. **select**

C. **delete**

D. **go to** the next line

1. **Look at page 130. *True* or *False*? Correct the underlined words in the false sentences.**

   a. The webcam is on top of the ~~printer~~. *monitor*   <u>   false   </u>

   b. The DVD and CD-ROM drive is in the <u>tower</u>.   _____

   c. The flash drive is in a <u>USB port</u>.   _____

   d. The power cord connects the tower to the <u>monitor</u>.   _____

   e. A <u>cable</u> connects the monitor to the keyboard.   _____

   f. The mouse is not connected to the <u>printer</u>.   _____

   g. Both computers have the same <u>software</u>.   _____

2. **Read Sara's email. Check (✓) the things Sara did.**

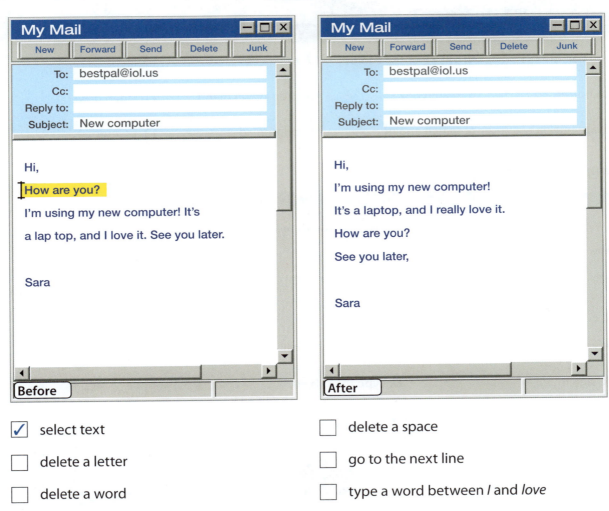

	My Mail ─ □ X
New	Forward	Send	Delete	Junk

To: bestpal@iol.us
Cc:
Reply to:
Subject: New computer

Hi,

How are you?

I'm using my new computer! It's a lap top, and I love it. See you later.

Sara

Before

	My Mail ─ □ X
New	Forward	Send	Delete	Junk

To: bestpal@iol.us
Cc:
Reply to:
Subject: New computer

Hi,

I'm using my new computer!

It's a laptop, and I really love it.

How are you?

See you later,

Sara

After

✓ select text	☐ delete a space
☐ delete a letter	☐ go to the next line
☐ delete a word	☐ type a word between *I* and *love*

See page 183 for listening practice.

The Internet

Navigating a Webpage

1. menu bar	4. URL / website address	7. tab	10. links	13. text box
2. back button	5. search box	8. drop-down menu	11. video player	14. cursor
3. forward button	6. search engine	9. pop-up ad	12. pointer	15. scroll ba

Logging on and Sending Email

A. type your password

B. click "sign in"

C. address the email

D. type the subject

E. type the message

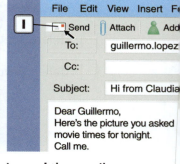

F. check your spelling

G. attach a picture

H. attach a file

I. send the email

1. Look at page 132. Match.

1. 2. I 3. 4.

_4_ **a.** back button   ___ **b.** pointer   ___ **c.** forward button   ___ **d.** cursor

2. What do you need to . . . ? Use the words in the box.

| scroll bar | ~~search box~~ | search engine | text box | video player |

a. look for information on the Web   __search box__ and _____

b. move up and down the screen   _____

c. type your password   _____

d. watch a movie on your computer   _____

3. Look at Todd's email. _True_ or _False_?

a. Todd addressed the email.   __true__   **d.** He attached a picture.   _____

b. He typed the subject.   _____   **e.** He attached a file.   _____

c. He typed the message in blue.   _____   **f.** He checked the spelling.   _____

4. What about you? Check (✓) the ways you use the Internet.

☐ send email   ☐ shop   ☐ pay bills   ☐ play online games

See page 183 for listening practice.

1. factory owner	5. parts	9. conveyer belt	13. pallet
2. designer	6. assembly line	10. order puller	14. shipping clerk
3. factory worker	7. warehouse	11. hand truck	15. loading dock
4. line supervisor	8. packer	12. forklift	

A. **design**

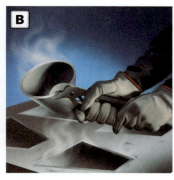

B. **manufacture**

C. **assemble**

D. **ship**

1. Look at page 134. *True* or *False*?

a. The factory manufactures lamps. _____true_____

b. The factory owner and the designer are in the warehouse. _____

c. A worker is operating a yellow forklift. _____

d. The line supervisor is pushing a hand truck. _____

e. There are three boxes on the pallet. _____

2. Cross out the word that doesn't belong.

a. **People**	designer	shipping clerk	~~forklift~~	packer
b. **Places**	factory owner	warehouse	factory	loading dock
c. **Machines**	hand truck	forklift	order puller	conveyor belt
d. **Jobs**	ship	parts	assemble	design

3. Complete the Lamplighter, Inc. job descriptions. Use the words in the box.

| ~~designer~~ | factory worker | line supervisor | order puller | packer | shipping clerk |

☀ LAMPLIGHTER, Inc.

a. design the lamp _____designer_____

b. watch the assembly line _____

c. assemble parts _____

d. count boxes on the loading dock _____

e. move boxes on a hand truck _____

f. put lamps in boxes on the conveyor belt _____

4. What about you? Look at the jobs in Exercise 3. Which one would you like? Which one wouldn't you like? Why?

Example: *I would like to be a line supervisor. I like to supervise people.*

See page 183 for listening practice.

Farming and Ranching

Crops

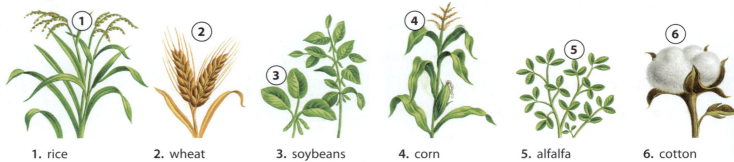

1. rice
2. wheat
3. soybeans
4. corn
5. alfalfa
6. cotton

A

B

C

D

7. field	12. farm equipment	17. corral	22. rancher
8. farmworker	13. farmer / grower	18. hay	A. **plant**
9. tractor	14. vegetable garden	19. fence	B. **harvest**
10. orchard	15. livestock	20. hired hand	C. **milk**
11. barn	16. vineyard	21. cattle	D. **feed**

1. **Look at page 136. Circle the words to complete the sentences.**

   a. A farmer / (rancher) is on a horse.

   b. In Picture C, a farmworker is milking / feeding a cow.

   c. There is hay / alfalfa near the fence of the corral.

   d. There is farm equipment / livestock next to the vegetable garden.

   e. A farmer is in the orchard / vineyard.

   f. In Picture B, two hired hands are harvesting / planting lettuce.

2. **Look at the bar graph. Number the crops in order. (1 = the biggest crop)**

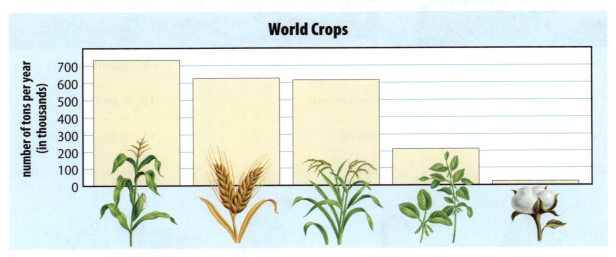

World Crops

number of tons per year (in thousands)

Based on information from: *Food and Agricultural Organization Statistical Yearbook, 2005–2006.*
http://www.fao.org/statistics/yearbook

____ a. wheat   ____ c. cotton   ____ e. soybeans

_1_ b. corn   ____ d. rice

3. **What about you? Have you ever been in . . . ? Check (✓) Yes or No.**

	Yes	No	If *yes*, where?
a. a field	☐	☐	_____
b. an orchard	☐	☐	_____
c. a barn	☐	☐	_____
d. a vineyard	☐	☐	_____
e. a vegetable garden	☐	☐	_____

See page 184 for listening practice.

Landscaping and Gardening

Bloom Nursery

1. gardening crew
2. leaf blower
3. wheelbarrow
4. gardening crew leader

5. landscape designer
6. lawn mower
7. shovel
8. rake

9. pruning shears
10. trowel
11. hedge clippers
12. weed whacker / weed eater

A. **mow** the lawn
B. **trim** the hedges

C. **rake** the leaves
D. **fertilize** / **feed** the plants

E. **plant** a tree
F. **water** the plants

G. **weed** the flower beds
H. **install** a sprinkler system

Use the new words.
Name what you can do in the garden.

A: *I can mow the lawn.*
B: *I can weed the flower bed.*

Ask your classmates. Share the answers.
1. Do you know someone who does landscaping? Who?
2. Do you enjoy gardening? Why or why not?
3. Which gardening activity is the hardest to do? Why?

1. **Look at page 138. *True* or *False*?**

   a. The gardening crew leader is talking to the landscape designer.   ___true___

   b. One of the gardening crew has a wheelbarrow.   _____

   c. The landscape designer is holding a leaf blower.   _____

   d. The shovel is between the lawn mower and the rake.   _____

   e. The pruning shears are to the right of the trowel.   _____

   f. The hedge clippers are to the left of the weed whacker.   _____

2. **Look at the Before and After pictures. Check (✓) the *completed* jobs.**

✓ install sprinkler system	☐ water the plants	☐ weed the flower beds
☐ plant trees	☐ mow the lawn	☐ trim the hedges
☐ fertilize the plants	☐ rake the leaves	

See page 184 for listening practice.   139

Trees and Plants

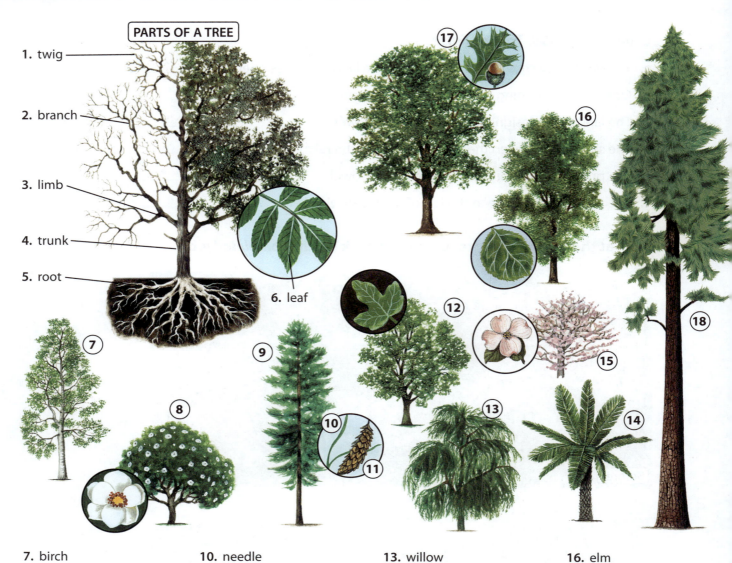

PARTS OF A TREE

1. twig
2. branch
3. limb
4. trunk
5. root
6. leaf

7. birch
8. magnolia
9. pine

10. needle
11. pinecone
12. maple

13. willow
14. palm
15. dogwood

16. elm
17. oak
18. redwood

Plants

19. holly
20. berries

21. cactus
22. vine

23. poison sumac
24. poison oak

25. poison ivy

1. **Look at page 140. *True* or *False*?**

    a. A tree has roots, limbs, branches, and twigs.   _____true_____

    b. Holly is a plant.   _____

    c. The birch tree has yellow leaves.   _____

    d. The magnolia and dogwood trees have flowers.   _____

    e. The cactus has berries.   _____

    f. Poison sumac has a trunk.   _____

    g. Poison ivy has three leaves.   _____

    h. The willow has pinecones.   _____

    i. A vine has needles.   _____

2. **Look at the bar graph. Number the trees in order of height. (1 = the tallest)**

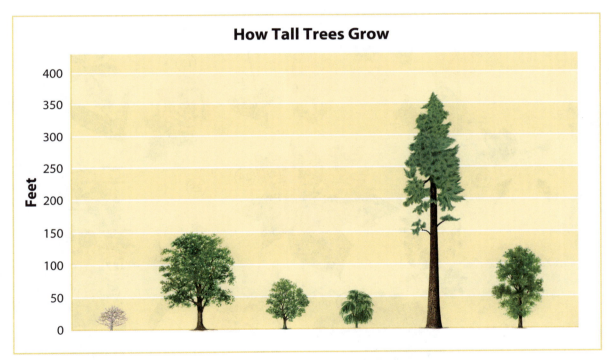

Based on information from: Petrides, G.: *Peterson Field Guides. Trees and Shrubs.*
(NY: Houghton Mifflin Co., 1986)

____ **a.** dogwood   ____ **d.** oak

____ **b.** elm   __1__ **e.** redwood

____ **c.** maple   ____ **f.** willow

See page 184 for listening practice.

Flowers

Parts of a Flower

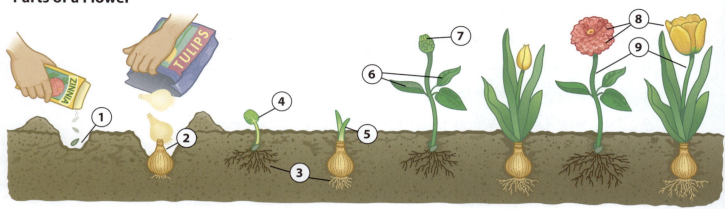

1. seed
2. bulb
3. roots

4. seedling
5. shoot
6. leaves

7. bud
8. petals
9. stems

10. sunflower
11. tulip
12. hibiscus
13. marigold
14. daisy

15. rose
16. iris
17. crocus
18. gardenia
19. orchid

20. carnation
21. chrysanthemum
22. jasmine
23. violet
24. poinsettia

25. daffodil
26. lily
27. houseplant
28. bouquet
29. thorn

1. **Look at page 142. Circle the words to complete the sentences.**

    a. The bouquet /(marigold) is orange.

    b. The tulip / crocus and the gardenia / poinsettia are red.

    c. The chrysanthemum / daffodil and the houseplant / lily are yellow.

    d. The carnation / jasmine and the daisy / orchid are white.

2. **What goes below the ground? What goes above the ground? Put the words in the box in the correct part of the diagram.**

    ~~bud~~   ~~bulb~~   leaves   petals   roots   seed   stems   thorn   shoot

    above the ground — *bud*

    below the ground — *bulb*

3. **Look at the pictures. Match the state name with the flower name. Use a map for help.**

    _3_ a. Kansas   1. iris

    ___ b. Illinois   2. rose

    ___ c. New York   3. sunflower

    ___ d. Tennessee   4. violet

    ___ e. Hawaii   5. hibiscus

4. **What about you? What flowers grow in your . . . ?**

    home _____   neighborhood _____   country _____

See page 185 for listening practice.

Construction

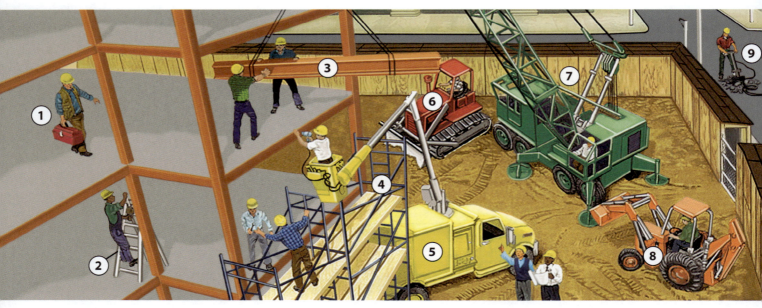

1. construction worker
2. ladder
3. I beam/girder

4. scaffolding
5. cherry picker
6. bulldozer

7. crane
8. backhoe
9. jackhammer / pneumatic drill

10. concrete
11. tile
12. bricks

13. trowel
14. insulation
15. stucco

16. window pane
17. wood / lumber
18. plywood

19. drywall
20. shingles
21. pickax

22. shovel
23. sledgehammer

A. **paint**

B. **lay** bricks

C. **install** tile

D. **hammer**

1. **Look at page 144. Put the words in the correct category.**

Heavy Machines	Tools	Building Material	
cherry picker	*jackhammer*	*concrete*	

Things To Stand On
ladder

2. **Look at the items. Match.**

__3__ a. | Install these tiles in the bathroom.

1.

_____ b. | Lay the bricks for the south wall.

2.

_____ c. | Hammer those nails into the wood.

3.

ADHESIVE

_____ d. | Paint it green.

4.

3. **What about you? Check (✓) the materials your school building has.**

☐ concrete   ☐ stucco

☐ shingles   ☐ tile

☐ bricks   ☐ wood

See page 185 for listening practice.

Tools and Building Supplies

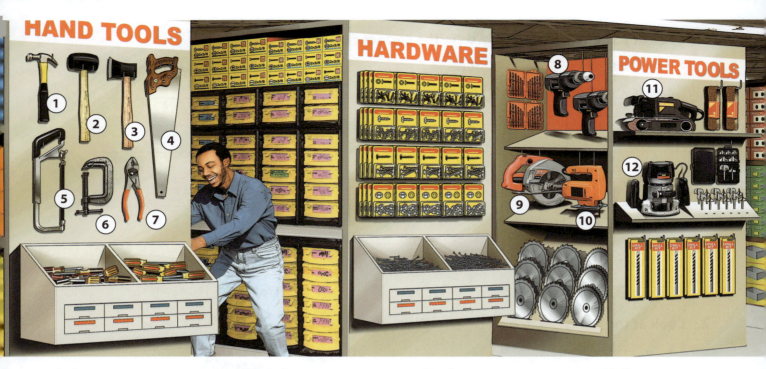

HAND TOOLS

HARDWARE

POWER TOOLS

1. hammer	**4.** handsaw	**7.** pliers	**10.** jigsaw
2. mallet	**5.** hacksaw	**8.** electric drill	**11.** power sander
3. ax	**6.** C-clamp	**9.** circular saw	**12.** router

26. vise	**30.** screwdriver	**34.** nail	**38.** toggle bolt
27. blade	**31.** Phillips screwdriver	**35.** bolt	**39.** hook
28. drill bit	**32.** machine screw	**36.** nut	**40.** eye hook
29. level	**33.** wood screw	**37.** washer	**41.** chain

Use the new words.
Look at pages 62–63. Name the tools you see.
A: *There's a hammer.*
B: *There's a pipe wrench.*

Ask your classmates. Share the answers.
1. Are you good with tools?
2. Which tools do you have at home?
3. Where can you shop for building supplies?

146

13. wire	16. yardstick	19. 2 x 4 (two by four)	22. paintbrush	25. paint
14. extension cord	17. pipe	20. particle board	23. paint roller	
15. bungee cord	18. fittings	21. spray gun	24. wood stain	

42. wire stripper	46. outlet cover	50. plunger	54. drop cloth
43. electrical tape	47. pipe wrench	51. paint pan	55. chisel
44. work light	48. adjustable wrench	52. scraper	56. sandpaper
45. tape measure	49. duct tape	53. masking tape	57. plane

Role play. Find an item in a building supply store.

A: *Where can I find particle board?*
B: *It's on the back wall, in the lumber section.*
A: *Great. And where underline{are the nails}?*

Think about it. Discuss.

1. Which tools are the most important to have? Why?
2. Which tools can be dangerous? Why?
3. Do you borrow tools from friends? Why or why not?

147

Tools and Building Supplies

1. Look at pages 146–147. Cross out the word that doesn't belong.

a. Hardware	nail	eye hook	~~outlet cover~~	wood screw
b. Plumbing	C-clamp	plunger	pipe	fittings
c. Power tools	circular saw	hammer	router	electric drill
d. Paint	wood stain	paint roller	spray gun	chisel
e. Electrical	wire stripper	plane	wire	extension cord
f. Hand tools	hacksaw	work light	pipe wrench	mallet

2. Look at the pictures. What do you need? Choose the correct tool from the box.

drill bit	~~electrical tape~~	level	paintbrush
Phillips screwdriver	sandpaper	scraper	screwdriver

a. <u>electrical tape</u>

b. _____

c. _____

d. _____

e. _____

f. _____

g. _____

h. _____

3. Look at the picture. How many . . . are there?

a. nuts <u>6</u>

b. nails ___

c. screws ___

d. washers ___

e. bolts ___

f. hooks ___

4. Look at the chart. *True* **or** *False*?

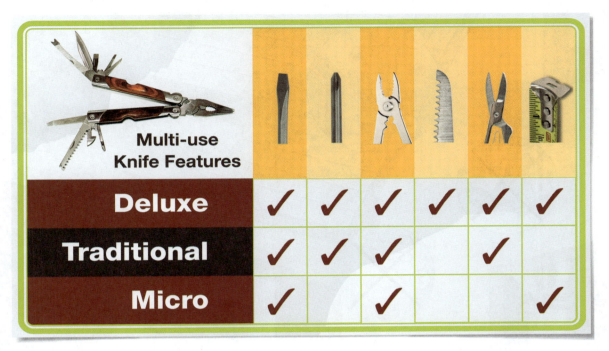

Multi-use Knife Features						
Deluxe	✓	✓	✓	✓	✓	✓
Traditional	✓	✓	✓		✓	
Micro	✓		✓			✓

a. The "Traditional" has a blade.   _____*false*_____

b. The "Micro" has a Phillips screwdriver.   _____

c. All three models have screwdrivers.   _____

d. All three models have a tape measure.   _____

e. The "Deluxe" has pliers.   _____

f. Only the "Deluxe" has a wire stripper.   _____

5. What about you? Check (✓) the tools and supplies you have.

☐ hammer

☐ handsaw

☐ power sander

☐ electric drill

☐ adjustable wrench

☐ jigsaw

☐ yardstick

☐ screwdriver

☐ plunger

☐ vise

☐ ax

☐ masking tape

☐ duct tape

☐ plane

☐ chisel

☐ Other: _____

See page 186 for listening practice.

1. The water heater is **not working**.

2. The power is **out**.

3. The roof is **leaking**.

4. The tile is **cracked**.

5. The window is **broken**.

6. The lock is **broken**.

7. The steps are **broken**.

8. roofer

9. electrician

10. repair person

11. locksmith

12. carpenter

13. fuse box

14. gas meter

More vocabulary

fix: to repair something that is broken
pests: termites, fleas, rats, etc.
exterminate: to kill household pests

Pair practice. Make new conversations.

A: *The faucet is* <u>leaking</u>.
B: *Let's call* <u>the plumber</u>. *He can fix it.*

5. The furnace is **broken**.

6. The pipes are **frozen**.

7. The faucet is **dripping**.

8. The sink is **overflowing**.

9. The toilet is **stopped up**.

20. plumber

21. exterminator

22. termites

23. ants

24. bedbugs

25. fleas

26. cockroaches / roaches

27. rats

28. mice*

*Note: one mouse, two mice

Ways to ask about repairs

How much will this repair cost?
When can you begin?
How long will the repair take?

Role play. Talk to a repair person.

A: *Can you fix the roof?*
B: *Yes, but it will take two weeks.*
A: *How much will the repair cost?*

1. **Look at pages 150–151. Who said . . . ?**

   a. I'm up on the roof. _____roofer_____

   b. Good-bye, termites! _____

   c. I'm turning on the power again. _____

   d. I'll fix the toilet next. _____

   e. I'm fixing the lock on the front door. _____

   f. There's one more step to repair. _____

   g. I'm putting in new windows. _____

2. **Look at John's bathroom. There are seven problems. Find and circle six more.**

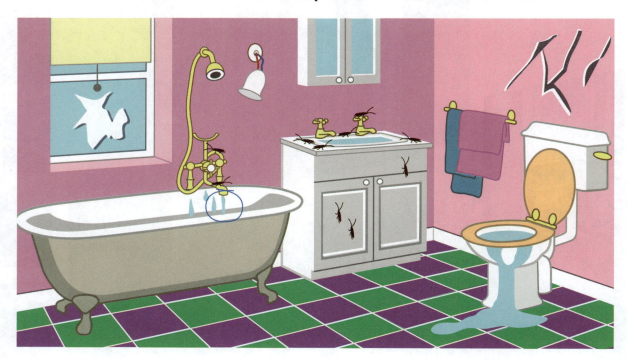

3. **Look at Exercise 2. *True* or *False*? Correct the <u>underlined</u> words in the false sentences.**

   a. The *bathtub* ~~sink~~ faucet is dripping. _____false_____

   b. The <u>window</u> is broken. _____

   c. There are <u>ants</u> near the sink. _____

   d. The <u>light</u> isn't working. _____

   e. The <u>sink</u> is overflowing. _____

   f. The <u>wall</u> is cracked. _____

4. Look at Exercise 2 and the ads below. Who should John call? Include the repair person, the problem(s), and the phone number on the list. (Hint: John will use some companies for more than one problem.)

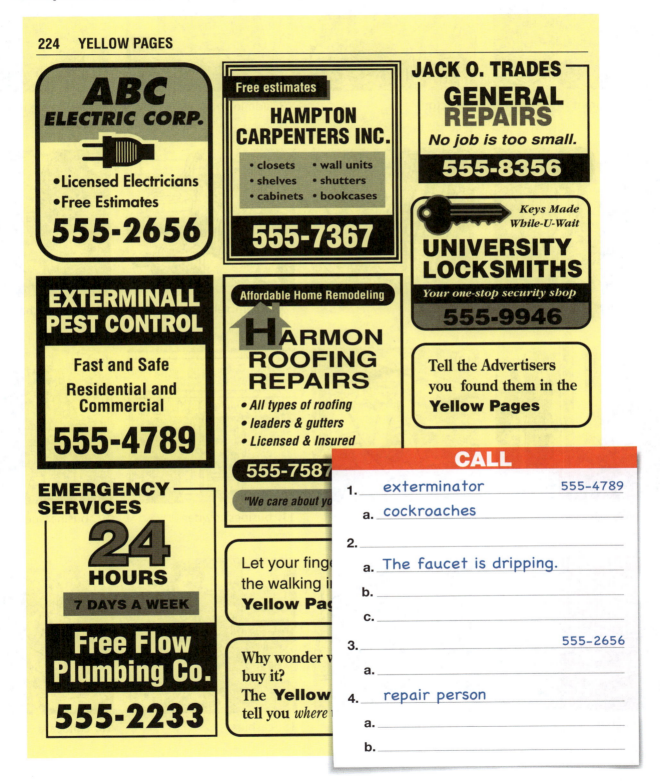

224   YELLOW PAGES

ABC ELECTRIC CORP.
- Licensed Electricians
- Free Estimates
555-2656

HAMPTON CARPENTERS INC.
Free estimates
- closets
- shelves
- cabinets
- wall units
- shutters
- bookcases
555-7367

JACK O. TRADES GENERAL REPAIRS
No job is too small.
555-8356

Keys Made While-U-Wait
UNIVERSITY LOCKSMITHS
Your one-stop security shop
555-9946

EXTERMINALL PEST CONTROL
Fast and Safe
Residential and Commercial
555-4789

Affordable Home Remodeling
HARMON ROOFING REPAIRS
- All types of roofing
- leaders & gutters
- Licensed & Insured
555-7587
"We care about yo...

Tell the Advertisers you found them in the **Yellow Pages**

EMERGENCY SERVICES
24 HOURS
7 DAYS A WEEK
Free Flow Plumbing Co.
555-2233

Let your finge...
the walking i...
Yellow Pag...

Why wonder w...
buy it?
The **Yellow**...
tell you *where*...

CALL
1. exterminator   555-4789
   a. cockroaches
2. _____
   a. The faucet is dripping.
   b. _____
   c. _____
3. _____   555-2656
   a. _____
4. repair person
   a. _____
   b. _____

See page 186 for listening practice.   153

1. accountant

2. actor

3. administrative assistant

4. appliance repair person

5. architect

6. artist

7. assembler

8. auto mechanic

9. babysitter

10. baker

11. business owner

12. businessperson

13. butcher

14. carpenter

15. cashier

16. childcare worker

Ways to ask about someone's job

What's her job?
What does he do?
What kind of work do they do?

Pair practice. Make new conversations.

A: *What kind of work <u>does she</u> do?*
B: <u>*She's an accountant*</u>. *What <u>do they</u> do?*
A: <u>*They're actors*</u>.

17. commercial fisher

18. computer software engineer

19. computer technician

We have that shirt in red.

20. customer service representative

21. delivery person

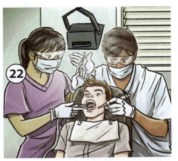

22. dental assistant

23. dockworker

24. electronics repair person

25. engineer

26. firefighter

27. florist

28. gardener

29. garment worker

30. graphic designer

31. hairdresser / hair stylist

32. home health care aide

Ways to talk about jobs and occupations

Sue's a garment worker. She works in a factory.
Tom's an engineer. He works for a large company.
Ann's a dental assistant. She works with a dentist.

Role play. Talk about a friend's new job.

A: *Does your friend like his new job?*
B: *Yes, he does. He's a graphic designer.*
A: *Does he work in an office?*

155

33. homemaker

34. housekeeper

你好

He says, "Hi."

35. interpreter / translator

36. lawyer

37. machine operator

38. manicurist

39. medical records technician

40. messenger / courier

41. model

42. mover

43. musician

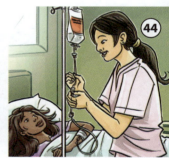

44. nurse

45. occupational therapist

46. (house) painter

47. physician assistant

48. police officer

Grammar Point: past tense of *be*

I **was** a machine operator for 5 years.
She **was** a nurse for a year.
They **were** movers from 2003–2007.

Pair practice. Make new conversations.

A: *What was your first job?*
B: *I was a musician. How about you?*
A: *I was a messenger for a small company.*

49. postal worker

50. printer

51. receptionist

52. reporter

53. retail clerk

54. sanitation worker

55. security guard

56. server

57. social worker

Here are some programs that will help you.

58. soldier

59. stock clerk

60. telemarketer

Hello. I'm calling with a very special offer.

61. truck driver

62. veterinarian

63. welder

64. writer / author

Ask your classmates. Share the answers.

1. Which of these jobs could you do now?
2. What is one job you don't want to have?
3. Which jobs do you want to have?

Think about it. Discuss.

1. Which jobs need special training?
2. What kind of person makes a good interpreter? A good nurse? A good reporter? Why?

Numbers

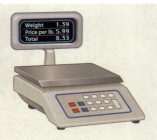

Cardinal Numbers

0	zero	20	twenty
1	one	21	twenty-one
2	two	22	twenty-two
3	three	23	twenty-three
4	four	24	twenty-four
5	five	25	twenty-five
6	six	30	thirty
7	seven	40	forty
8	eight	50	fifty
9	nine	60	sixty
10	ten	70	seventy
11	eleven	80	eighty
12	twelve	90	ninety
13	thirteen	100	one hundred
14	fourteen	101	one hundred one
15	fifteen	1,000	one thousand
16	sixteen	10,000	ten thousand
17	seventeen	100,000	one hundred thousand
18	eighteen	1,000,000	one million
19	nineteen	1,000,000,000	one billion

Ordinal Numbers

1st	first	16th	sixteenth
2nd	second	17th	seventeenth
3rd	third	18th	eighteenth
4th	fourth	19th	nineteenth
5th	fifth	20th	twentieth
6th	sixth	21st	twenty-first
7th	seventh	30th	thirtieth
8th	eighth	40th	fortieth
9th	ninth	50th	fiftieth
10th	tenth	60th	sixtieth
11th	eleventh	70th	seventieth
12th	twelfth	80th	eightieth
13th	thirteenth	90th	ninetieth
14th	fourteenth	100th	one hundredth
15th	fifteenth	1,000th	one thousandth

Roman Numerals

I = 1	VII = 7	XXX = 30
II = 2	VIII = 8	XL = 40
III = 3	IX = 9	L = 50
IV = 4	X = 10	C = 100
V = 5	XV = 15	D = 500
VI = 6	XX = 20	M = 1,000

A 1 ÷ 4 = .25

A. divide

B 75% of 10 = 7.5

B. calculate

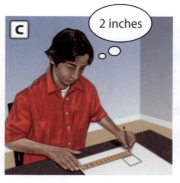
C 2 inches

C. measure

D 1 mi. = 1.6 km

1 MILE TO LAKE

D. convert

Fractions and Decimals

1

1. one whole
1 = 1.00

2

2. one half
1/2 = .5

3

3. one third
1/3 = .333

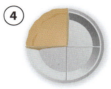
4

4. one fourth
1/4 = .25

5

5. one eighth
1/8 = .125

Percents

6

6. calculator

7. decimal point

7

8. 100 percent — 100%
9. 75 percent — 75%
10. 50 percent — 50%
11. 25 percent — 25%
12. 10 percent — 10%

0% 10% 20% 30% 40% 50% 60% 70% 80% 90% 100%

Measurement

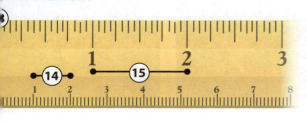

13. ruler
14. centimeter [cm]
15. inch [in.]

Dimensions

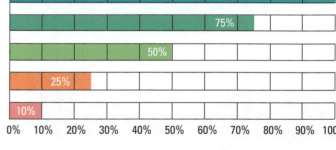

16. height
17. length
18. depth
19. width

Equivalencies

12 inches = 1 foot
3 feet = 1 yard
1,760 yards = 1 mile
1 inch = 2.54 centimeters
1 yard = .91 meters
1 mile = 1.6 kilometers

Telling Time

1. hour

2. minutes

3. seconds

4. a.m.

5. p.m.

6. 1:00
one o'clock

7. 1:05
one-oh-five
five after one

8. 1:10
one-ten
ten after one

9. 1:15
one-fifteen
a quarter after one

10. 1:20
one-twenty
twenty after one

11. 1:30
one-thirty
half past one

12. 1:40
one-forty
twenty to two

13. 1:45
one-forty-five
a quarter to two

Times of Day

14. sunrise

15. morning

16. noon

17. afternoon

18. sunset

19. evening

20. night

21. midnight

Ways to talk about time

I wake up at 6:30 a.m.
I wake up at 6:30 in the morning.
I wake up at 6:30.

Pair practice. Make new conversations.

A: *What time do you wake up on weekdays?*
B: *At 6:30 a.m. How about you?*
A: *I wake up at 7:00.*

SCHEDULED STOPS	TO MIDTOWN TERMINAL
Oak Street	9:00 AM
Tramont Street	
Canyon Blvd.	9
Briargate Blvd.	9:2
Pierceton Drive	9:28 A
Columbus Blvd.	9:35 A

22. early   **23.** on time   **24.** late

25. daylight saving time   **26.** standard time

Time Zones

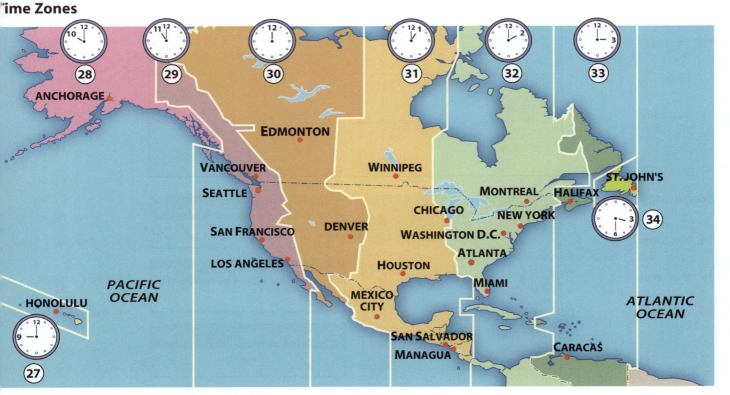

27. Hawaii-Aleutian time   **29.** Pacific time   **31.** Central time   **33.** Atlantic time

28. Alaska time   **30.** Mountain time   **32.** Eastern time   **34.** Newfoundland time

---

Ask your classmates. Share the answers.

1. When do you watch television? study? relax?
2. Do you like to stay up after midnight?
3. Do you like to wake up late on weekends?

Think about it. Discuss.

1. What is your favorite time of day? Why?
2. Do you think daylight saving time is a good idea? Why or why not?

161

The Calendar

1. date
2. day
3. month
4. year

5. today
6. tomorrow
7. yesterday

Days of the Week

8. Sunday
9. Monday
10. Tuesday
11. Wednesday
12. Thursday
13. Friday
14. Saturday

15. week
16. weekdays
17. weekend

MAY

SUN	MON	TUE	WED	THU	FRI	SAT
1	2	3	4	5	6	7
8	9	10	11	12	13	14
15	16	17	18	19	20	21
22	23	24	25	26	27	28
29	30	31				

Frequency

18. last week
19. this week
20. next week

MAY

SUN	MON	TUE	WED	THU	FRI	SAT
1	2	3	4	5	6	7
8	9	10	11	12	13	14
15	16	17	18	19	20	21
22	23	24	25	26	27	28

21. every day / daily
22. once a week
23. twice a week
24. three times a week

Ways to say the date

Today is May 10th. It's the tenth.
Yesterday was May 9th.
The party is on May 21st.

Pair practice. Make new conversations.

A: *The test is on Friday, June 14th.*
B: *Did you say Friday, the fourteenth?*
A: *Yes, the fourteenth.*

Months of the Year

㉕ JAN
SUN	MON	TUE	WED	THU	FRI	SAT
					1	2
3	4	5	6	7	8	9
10	11	12	13	14	15	16
17	18	19	20	21	22	23
24/31	25	26	27	28	29	30

㉖ FEB
SUN	MON	TUE	WED	THU	FRI	SAT
	1	2	3	4	5	6
7	8	9	10	11	12	13
14	15	16	17	18	19	20
21	22	23	24	25	26	27
28						

㉗ MAR
SUN	MON	TUE	WED	THU	FRI	SAT
	1	2	3	4	5	6
7	8	9	10	11	12	13
14	15	16	17	18	19	20
21	22	23	24	25	26	27
28	29	30	31			

㉘ APR
SUN	MON	TUE	WED	THU	FRI	SAT
				1	2	3
4	5	6	7	8	9	10
11	12	13	14	15	16	17
18	19	20	21	22	23	24
25	26	27	28	29	30	

㉙ MAY
SUN	MON	TUE	WED	THU	FRI	SAT
						1
2	3	4	5	6	7	8
9	10	11	12	13	14	15
16	17	18	19	20	21	22
23/30	24/31	25	26	27	28	29

㉚ JUN
SUN	MON	TUE	WED	THU	FRI	SAT
		1	2	3	4	5
6	7	8	9	10	11	12
13	14	15	16	17	18	19
20	21	22	23	24	25	26
27	28	29	30			

㉛ JUL
SUN	MON	TUE	WED	THU	FRI	SAT
				1	2	3
4	5	6	7	8	9	10
11	12	13	14	15	16	17
18	19	20	21	22	23	24
25	26	27	28	29	30	31

㉜ AUG
SUN	MON	TUE	WED	THU	FRI	SAT
1	2	3	4	5	6	7
8	9	10	11	12	13	14
15	16	17	18	19	20	21
22	23	24	25	26	27	28
29	30	31				

㉝ SEP
SUN	MON	TUE	WED	THU	FRI	SAT
			1	2	3	4
5	6	7	8	9	10	11
12	13	14	15	16	17	18
19	20	21	22	23	24	25
26	27	28	29	30		

㉞ OCT
SUN	MON	TUE	WED	THU	FRI	SAT
					1	2
3	4	5	6	7	8	9
10	11	12	13	14	15	16
17	18	19	20	21	22	23
24/31	25	26	27	28	29	30

㉟ NOV
SUN	MON	TUE	WED	THU	FRI	SAT
	1	2	3	4	5	6
7	8	9	10	11	12	13
14	15	16	17	18	19	20
21	22	23	24	25	26	27
28	29	30				

㊱ DEC
SUN	MON	TUE	WED	THU	FRI	SAT
			1	2	3	4
5	6	7	8	9	10	11
12	13	14	15	16	17	18
19	20	21	22	23	24	25
26	27	28	29	30	31	

Months of the Year

25. January

26. February

27. March

28. April

29. May

30. June

31. July

32. August

33. September

34. October

35. November

36. December

Seasons

37. spring

38. summer

39. fall / autumn

40. winter

Dictate to your partner. Take turns.

A: *Write Monday.*

B: *Is it spelled M-o-n-d-a-y?*

A: *Yes, that's right.*

Ask your classmates. Share the answers.

1. What is your favorite day of the week? Why?
2. What is your busiest day of the week? Why?
3. What is your favorite season of the year? Why?

Describing Things

1. **little** hand

2. **big** hand

13. **heavy** box

14. **light** box

3. **fast** driver

4. **slow** driver

15. **same** color

16. **different** colors

5. **hard** chair

6. **soft** chair

17. **good** dog

18. **bad** dog

7. **thick** book

8. **thin** book

19. **expensive** ring

20. **cheap** ring

9. **full** glass

10. **empty** glass

21. **beautiful** view
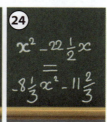 
22. **ugly** view

11. **noisy** children / **loud** children

12. **quiet** children

23. **easy** problem
 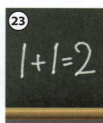
24. **difficult** problem / **hard** problem

Ask your classmates. Share the answers.
1. Are you a slow driver or a fast driver?
2. Do you prefer a hard bed or a soft bed?
3. Do you like loud parties or quiet parties?

Use the new words.
Look at a street nearby. Describe the things you see.

A: _The street_ is hard.
B: _The truck_ is _heavy_.

Coins

1. $.01 = 1¢
a penny / 1 cent

3. $.10 = 10¢
a dime / 10 cents

5. $.50 = 50¢
a half dollar

2. $.05 = 5¢
a nickel / 5 cents

4. $.25 = 25¢
a quarter / 25 cents

6. $1.00
a dollar coin

Bills

7. $1.00
a dollar

8. $5.00
five dollars

9. $10.00
ten dollars

10. $20.00
twenty dollars

11. $50.00
fifty dollars

12. $100.00
one hundred dollars

A. Get change.

B. Borrow money.   **C. Lend** money.

D. Pay back the money.

Pair practice. Make new conversations.

A: *Do you have change for a dollar?*
B: *Sure. How about two quarters and five dimes?*
A: *Perfect!*

Think about it. Discuss.

1. Is it a good idea to lend money to a friend? Why or why not?
2. Is it better to carry a dollar or four quarters? Why?
3. Do you prefer dollar coins or dollar bills? Why?

165

Listening Exercises

 Job Skills pages 2–3

Listen. Check (✓) Andrea's job skills.

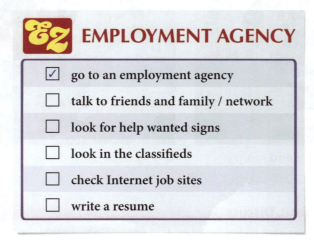

Ron's Roadside Restaurant

JOB SKILLS

- ✓ cook
- ☐ wait on customers
- ☐ use a cash register
- ☐ speak another language
- ☐ supervise people
- ☐ repair appliances

 Personal Information pages 4–5

Listen. Check (✓) the answers.

1. ☐ **a.** Ana   ✓ **b.** Garcia
2. ☐ **a.** 212   ☐ **b.** 10003-1100
3. ☐ **a.** Mexico City   ☐ **b.** 4/6/90
4. ☐ **a.** 10   ☐ **b.** 401-555-0323
5. ☐ **a.** 534-12-0000   ☐ **b.** 1-(917)-555-0747
6. ☐ **a.** Ana Garcia   ☐ **b.** *Ana Garcia*

Ana Garcia

 Job Search pages 6–7

Listen. Check (✓) the things Amy does to find a job.

EZ EMPLOYMENT AGENCY

- ✓ go to an employment agency
- ☐ talk to friends and family / network
- ☐ look for help wanted signs
- ☐ look in the classifieds
- ☐ check Internet job sites
- ☐ write a resume

Interview Skills   pages 8–9

Listen. *True* or *False*? Check (✓) the answers.

	True	False
1. Roger dressed appropriately for his interview.	✓	☐
2. He greeted the interviewer.	☐	☐
3. He brought his resume.	☐	☐
4. He turned off his cell phone before the interview.	☐	☐
5. He asked questions.	☐	☐
6. He thanked the interviewer.	☐	☐

Everyday Conversation   pages 10–11

Listen. *True* or *False*? Check (✓) the answers.

	True	False
1. He's explaining something.	✓	☐
2. They disagree.	☐	☐
3. She's complimenting someone.	☐	☐
4. She's accepting an invitation.	☐	☐
5. He's offering something.	☐	☐
6. They're checking their understanding.	☐	☐
7. He's apologizing.	☐	☐
8. He's thanking someone.	☐	☐

The Workplace   pages 12–15

Look at pages 12–13. Listen. Who are they looking for? Check (✓) the answers.

1. ☐ **a.** employer   ✓ **b.** receptionist
2. ☐ **a.** payroll clerk   ☐ **b.** supervisor
3. ☐ **a.** customer   ☐ **b.** supervisor
4. ☐ **a.** receptionist   ☐ **b.** supervisor
5. ☐ **a.** boss   ☐ **b.** employee

Workplace Clothing pages 16–19

Listen. Check (✓) the items the people want to buy.

1. ☑ safety glasses
   ☑ apron
   ☐ chef's hat
   ☐ waist apron
   ☑ bump cap

2. ☐ work shirt
   ☐ work gloves
   ☐ work pants
   ☐ bandana
   ☐ latex gloves

3. ☐ safety glasses
   ☐ security pants
   ☐ security shirt
   ☐ work pants
   ☐ polo shirt

4. ☐ cowboy hat
   ☐ ventilation mask
   ☐ hard hat
   ☐ blazer
   ☐ steel toe boots

5. ☐ helmet
   ☐ latex gloves
   ☐ hairnets
   ☐ disposable gloves
   ☐ smock

6. ☐ face mask
   ☐ scrubs
   ☐ ventilation mask
   ☐ lab coat
   ☐ surgical mask

7. ☐ coveralls
   ☐ lab coat
   ☐ scrubs
   ☐ latex gloves
   ☐ jumpsuit

Job Safety pages 20–21

Listen. What are the workers using or wearing? Check (✓) the answers.

1. ☑ a. ear plugs   ☐ b. knee pads
2. ☐ a. ear muffs   ☐ b. two-way radio
3. ☐ a. respirator   ☐ b. work gloves
4. ☐ a. safety boots   ☐ b. safety goggles
5. ☐ a. hard hat   ☐ b. fire extinguisher

A Hotel pages 22–23

Look at page 22. Who said . . . ? Circle the answers.

1. a. bell hop   (b.) parking attendant
2. a. desk clerk   b. doorman
3. a. bell captain   b. concierge
4. a. pool service   b. maintenance
5. a. guest   b. housekeeper
6. a. concierge   b. maintenance

Housework   pages 24–25

Listen. What are the people doing? Check (✓) the answers.

1. ☐ **a.** drying the dishes   ✓ **b.** changing the sheets
2. ☐ **a.** putting away toys   ☐ **b.** recycling the newspapers
3. ☐ **a.** mopping the floor   ☐ **b.** vacuuming the carpet
4. ☐ **a.** washing the dishes   ☐ **b.** washing the windows
5. ☐ **a.** polishing the furniture   ☐ **b.** wiping the counter
6. ☐ **a.** putting away the toys   ☐ **b.** taking out the garbage
7. ☐ **a.** dusting the furniture   ☐ **b.** making the bed

Cleaning Supplies   pages 26–27

Listen. Look at the list. Check (✓) the things they need.

To Buy

☑ glass cleaner   ☐ furniture polish
☐ cleanser   ☐ oven cleaner
☐ sponges   ☐ steel-wool soap pads
☐ scrub brush   ☐ trash bags
☐ dishwashing liquid   ☐ bucket

Doing the Laundry   pages 28–29

Listen. *True* or *False*? Check (✓) the answers.

	True	False
1. They're sorting the laundry.	✓	☐
2. He's adding the detergent.	☐	☐
3. She's ironing the clothes.	☐	☐
4. She's folding the laundry.	☐	☐
5. He's cleaning the lint trap.	☐	☐
6. He's unloading the dryer.	☐	☐
7. She's loading the washer.	☐	☐

Food Service pages 30–31

Look at page 30. Listen. *True* or *False*? Check (✓) the answers.

	True	False
1.	☐	✓
2.	☐	☐
3.	☐	☐
4.	☐	☐
5.	☐	☐
6.	☐	☐

Kitchen Utensils pages 32–33

Look at page 32. Listen. *True* or *False*? Check (✓) the answers.

	True	False
1.	✓	☐
2.	☐	☐
3.	☐	☐
4.	☐	☐
5.	☐	☐
6.	☐	☐
7.	☐	☐

A Restaurant pages 34–37

Listen. Who said . . . ? Circle the answers.

1. the busser / the hostess
2. the chef / a server
3. the busser / a patron
4. the dishwasher / the hostess
5. the busser / the chef
6. a waiter / a waitress
7. a diner / a server
8. the busser / the hostess

A Fast Food Restaurant   pages 38–39

Look at page 38. Listen. Who said . . . ? Check (✓) the columns.

	Counterperson	Customers at the Counter	Cook	Customers at the Table
1.		✓		
2.				
3.				
4.				
5.				
6.				
7.				

 A Coffee Shop Menu   pages 40–43

Listen. Complete the orders.

1.
Coffee Shop
ORDER FORM

pancakes
_____
_____
_____
_____

2.
Coffee Shop
ORDER FORM

_____
_____
_____
_____

3.
Coffee Shop
ORDER FORM

_____
_____
_____
_____

4.
Coffee Shop
ORDER FORM

_____
_____
_____
_____

Food Preparation and Safety   pages 44–47

**Look at the pictures. Listen to the recipe. Number the pictures in order.
(1 = the first step)**

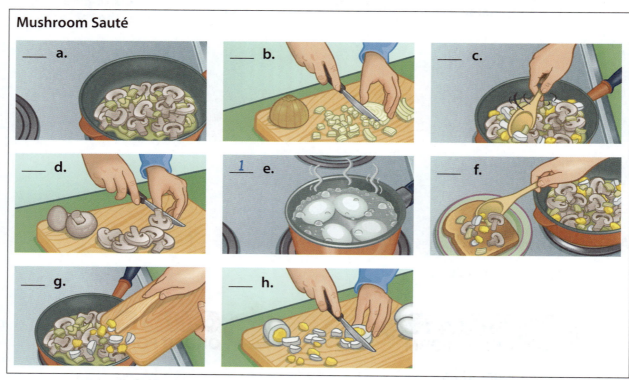

Mushroom Sauté

_____ a.

_____ b.

_____ c.

_____ d.

_1_ e.

_____ f.

_____ g.

_____ h.

Based on a recipe from: Richmond, S. *International Vegetarian Cooking.* (NY: Arco Publishing Co., 1970)

A Grocery Store   pages 48–51

Listen. Write the aisle numbers.

	Aisle
aluminum foil	____
apple juice	____
bagels	____
canned beans	_6_
coffee	____
ice cream	____
yogurt	____

Seafood and Deli pages 52–53

Listen. Complete the orders. Check (✓) the food the people order.

1.
ORDER FORM

Dan's
DELI SANDWICHES

Meat/Poultry
- ✓ roast beef
- ☐ corned beef
- ☐ salami
- ☐ pastrami
- ☐ smoked turkey

Cheese
- ☐ American
- ☐ Swiss
- ☐ cheddar
- ☐ mozzarella

Bread
- ☐ rye
- ☐ white
- ☐ wheat

2.
ORDER FORM

Dan's
DELI SANDWICHES

Meat/Poultry
- ☐ roast beef
- ☐ corned beef
- ☐ salami
- ☐ pastrami
- ☐ smoked turkey

Cheese
- ☐ American
- ☐ Swiss
- ☐ cheddar
- ☐ mozzarella

Bread
- ☐ rye
- ☐ white
- ☐ wheat

3.
ORDER FORM

Dan's
DELI SANDWICHES

Meat/Poultry
- ☐ roast beef
- ☐ corned beef
- ☐ salami
- ☐ pastrami
- ☐ smoked turkey

Cheese
- ☐ American
- ☐ Swiss
- ☐ cheddar
- ☐ mozzarella

Bread
- ☐ rye
- ☐ white
- ☐ wheat

4.
ORDER FORM

Dan's
DELI SANDWICHES

Meat/Poultry
- ☐ roast beef
- ☐ corned beef
- ☐ salami
- ☐ pastrami
- ☐ smoked turkey

Cheese
- ☐ American
- ☐ Swiss
- ☐ cheddar
- ☐ mozzarella

Bread
- ☐ rye
- ☐ white
- ☐ wheat

Containers and Packaging pages 54–55

Listen. Match.

__f__ **1.** bag

____ **2.** bottle

____ **3.** container

____ **4.** box

____ **5.** can

____ **6.** six-pack

____ **7.** package

a. juice

b. soda

c. pasta

d. water

e. cookies

f. nuts

g. yogurt

Weights and Measurements   pages 56–57

Listen. Circle the words you hear.

1. a pint / (a quart)
2. a teaspoon / a tablespoon
3. a cup / a quart
4. a pint / a gallon
5. two teaspoons / two tablespoons
6. two ounces / three ounces

A Mall   pages 58–61

Look at pages 58–59. *True* or *False*? Check (✓) the answers.

	True	False			True	False
1.	✓	☐		5.	☐	☐
2.	☐	☐		6.	☐	☐
3.	☐	☐		7.	☐	☐
4.	☐	☐				

Shopping   pages 62–63

Listen. *True* or *False*? Check (✓) the answers.

		True	False
1.	She wants to buy the lamp.	☐	✓
2.	She wants to exchange it.	☐	☐
3.	She used a debit card.	☐	☐
4.	She has the receipt.	☐	☐
5.	He wants to return a lamp.	☐	☐
6.	The sale price is $20.00	☐	☐
7.	There's sales tax.	☐	☐
8.	He's going to write a check.	☐	☐

Colors pages 64–65

Listen. *True* or *False*? Check (✓) the answers.

	True	False			True	False
1.	✓	☐	2.		☐	☐
3.	☐	☐	4.		☐	☐
5.	☐	☐	6.		☐	☐

 Prepositions pages 66–67

Listen. Circle the words to complete the sentences.

1. The red sweaters are on the left / right.
2. The blue sweaters are below / behind the white sweaters.
3. The green sweaters are above / under the black sweaters.
4. The white sweaters are behind / between the pink sweaters and the orange sweaters.
5. The gray sweaters are in / on the box over there.
6. The purple sweaters are on the left / right.
7. The yellow sweaters are in front of / next to the orange sweaters.

 Everyday Clothes pages 68–71

Look at pages 68–69. Who said . . . ? Circle the answers.

1. the man in jeans / the suit
2. the woman with the handbag / sweater
3. the person in the baseball cap / tan slacks
4. the man in the blue shirt / suit
5. the woman wearing a skirt / yellow dress
6. the man wearing a T-shirt / jeans
7. the man in the blue / green shirt

Casual, Work, and Formal Clothes pages 72–75

Listen. *True* or *False*? Check (✓) the answers.

	True	False
1. She wears a uniform to work.	✓	☐
2. He wears sweatpants and a tank top at the gym.	☐	☐
3. She's going to wear a cocktail dress.	☐	☐
4. She's going to wear capris and sandals.	☐	☐
5. He's going to wear a tuxedo.	☐	☐
6. He's going to wear a sports jacket.	☐	☐
7. She's going to take a cardigan sweater.	☐	☐

Seasonal Clothing pages 76–77

Listen. Write the floor number.

DIRECTORY	FLOOR	DIRECTORY	FLOOR
coats	_____	rain boots	_____
gloves	_____	sunglasses	_____
hats	_____	swimsuits	5
leggings	_____	umbrellas	_____

Shoes and Accessories pages 78–81

Look at the top picture on pages 78–79. Listen. Who said . . . ? Circle the answers.

1. the salesclerk in the jewelry department / near the belts
2. the woman with the backpack / shoulder bag
3. the customer in the jewelry / shoe department
4. the salesclerk near the wallet display case / in the jewelry department
5. the man looking at rings / waiting in line
6. the man purchasing a shirt / shoes
7. the woman assisting a customer / purchasing shoes

Describing Clothes   pages 82–85

Listen. What is the problem? Check (✓) the answers.

1. ☐ **a.** A button is missing.   ✓ **b.** The zipper is broken.
2. ☐ **a.** They're too light.   ☐ **b.** They're too tight.
3. ☐ **a.** They're too wide.   ☐ **b.** They're too high.
4. ☐ **a.** It's stained.   ☐ **b.** It's torn.
5. ☐ **a.** It's too heavy.   ☐ **b.** It's too fancy.
6. ☐ **a.** It's too small.   ☐ **b.** It's too big.
7. ☐ **a.** They're too low.   ☐ **b.** They're too loose.

Making Clothes   pages 86–89

Listen. Circle the words to complete the sentences.

1. It's a cotton / wool sweater.
2. The man wants leather / suede shoes.
3. The woman wants a lace / silk camisole.
4. The woman loves cashmere / velvet.
5. It's a linen / nylon jacket.
6. The dress closes with a snap / zipper.
7. The woman likes the beads / fringe.

Making Alterations pages 90–91

Listen. Check (✓) the things the tailor will do.

1. ## Tailor Made
Quality Tailoring Repairs and Alterations

CLOTHING	ALTERATIONS	REPAIR
✓ pants	☐ lengthen	☐ collar
☐ shirt (sleeves)	✓ shorten	☐ waistband
	☐ let out	☐ sleeve
☐ skirt	✓ take in	✓ pocket

2. ## Tailor Made
Quality Tailoring Repairs and Alterations

CLOTHING	ALTERATIONS	REPAIR
☐ pants	☐ lengthen	☐ collar
☐ shirt (sleeves)	☐ shorten	☐ waistband
	☐ let out	☐ sleeve
☐ skirt	☐ take in	☐ pocket

3. ## Tailor Made
Quality Tailoring Repairs and Alterations

CLOTHING	ALTERATIONS	REPAIR
☐ pants	☐ lengthen	☐ collar
☐ shirt (sleeves)	☐ shorten	☐ waistband
	☐ let out	☐ sleeve
☐ skirt	☐ take in	☐ pocket

4. ## Tailor Made
Quality Tailoring Repairs and Alterations

CLOTHING	ALTERATIONS	REPAIR
☐ pants	☐ lengthen	☐ collar
☐ shirt (sleeves)	☐ shorten	☐ waistband
	☐ let out	☐ sleeve
☐ skirt	☐ take in	☐ pocket

 Describing Hair pages 92–93

Listen. What do the people want? Check (✓) the answers.

1. ☐ **a.** color ✓ **b.** cut
2. ☐ **a.** bangs ☐ **b.** part
3. ☐ **a.** black ☐ **b.** brown
4. ☐ **a.** blond ☐ **b.** red
5. ☐ **a.** straight hair ☐ **b.** wavy hair
6. ☐ **a.** shoulder-length hair ☐ **b.** short hair
7. ☐ **a.** color his beard ☐ **b.** color his mustache
8. ☐ **a.** perm ☐ **b.** set

Electronics and Photography   pages 94–97

Listen. What are they using? Check (✓) the answers.

1. ☐ **a.** speakers   ✓ **b.** universal remote
2. ☐ **a.** portable DVD Player ☐ **b.** tripod
3. ☐ **a.** adapter   ☐ **b.** MP3 player
4. ☐ **a.** digital camera   ☐ **b.** photo album
5. ☐ **a.** battery pack   ☐ **b.** film
6. ☐ **a.** camera case   ☐ **b.** zoom lens

The Hospital   pages 98–101

Look at page 98. Who said . . . ? Check (✓) the answers.

1. ✓ **a.** obstetrician   ☐ **b.** oncologist
2. ☐ **a.** cardiologist   ☐ **b.** pediatrician
3. ☐ **a.** ophthalmologist   ☐ **b.** radiologist
4. ☐ **a.** psychiatrist   ☐ **b.** registered nurse
5. ☐ **a.** dietician   ☐ **b.** surgical nurse
6. ☐ **a.** internist   ☐ **b.** orderly
7. ☐ **a.** certified nursing assistant   ☐ **b.** administrator

Inside and Outside the Body   pages 102–105

Listen. What is the teacher talking about? Check (✓) the answers.

1. ✓ **a.** skin   ☐ **b.** shin
2. ☐ **a.** gums   ☐ **b.** lungs
3. ☐ **a.** brain   ☐ **b.** bone
4. ☐ **a.** skeleton   ☐ **b.** skull
5. ☐ **a.** thumb   ☐ **b.** tongue
6. ☐ **a.** bladder   ☐ **b.** gallbladder
7. ☐ **a.** knees   ☐ **b.** kidneys

Symptoms and Injuries pages 106–107

Listen. Complete the medical chart. Check (✓) the symptoms.

✦ MEDICAL CENTER

Dr. Eng

10 Oak Drive, Richmond, CA

DATE: 3/5

PATIENT'S NAME: *Enrique Rivera*

✓ sore throat	☐ stomachache	☐ cough
☐ nasal congestion	☐ toothache	☐ sneeze
☐ fever	☐ earache	☐ feel dizzy
☐ chills	☐ headache	☐ feel nauseous
☐ rash	☐ backache	☐ throw up

 Illnesses and Medical Conditions pages 108–109

Listen. Check (✓) the illness or medical condition.

1. ✓ **a.** flu   ☐ **b.** cold
2. ☐ **a.** ear infection   ☐ **b.** strep throat
3. ☐ **a.** allergies   ☐ **b.** asthma
4. ☐ **a.** measles   ☐ **b.** mumps
5. ☐ **a.** HIV   ☐ **b.** TB
6. ☐ **a.** diabetes   ☐ **b.** dementia
7. ☐ **a.** heart disease   ☐ **b.** hypertension

 Medical Emergencies pages 110–111

Listen. *True* or *False*? Check (✓) the answers.

	True	False		True	False
1. He burned himself.	✓	☐	5. Susan is unconscious.	☐	☐
2. She got frostbite.	☐	☐	6. He swallowed poison.	☐	☐
3. He's bleeding.	☐	☐	7. She got an electric shock.	☐	☐
4. She's choking.	☐	☐			

First Aid pages 112–113

Listen. Check (✓) the items inside the first aid kit.

⚕ FIRST AID KIT

- ☐ tweezers
- ☑ adhesive bandages
- ☐ sterile pads
- ☐ sterile tape
- ☐ gauze

- ☐ hydrogen peroxide
- ☐ antibacterial ointment
- ☐ antihistamine cream
- ☐ elastic bandages
- ☐ ice pack

Medical Care pages 114–115

Look at page 114. Listen. Who said . . . ? Check (✓) the columns.

	Patient	Doctor	Nurse	Receptionist
1.			✓	
2.				
3.				
4.				
5.				
6.				
7.				

A Pharmacy pages 116–119

Listen. Write the number of the conversation.

___ a.

___ b.

___ c.

_1_ d.

___ e.

Personal Hygiene   pages 120–123

Listen. What are they doing? Circle the words to complete the sentences.

1. She's <u>combing</u> / (washing) her hair.

2. She's <u>polishing</u> / <u>cutting</u> her nails.

3. He's brushing his <u>hair / teeth</u>.

4. He's <u>shaving</u> / <u>using deodorant</u>.

5. She's <u>drying</u> / <u>rinsing</u> her hair.

6. He's <u>gargling</u> / <u>taking a bath</u>.

7. She's <u>putting on</u> / <u>taking off</u> mascara.

Office Skills   pages 124–125

Listen. *True* or *False*? Check (✓) the answers.

	True	False
1. He's typing.	✓	☐
2. She's leaving a message.	☐	☐
3. He's faxing a document.	☐	☐
4. She's putting the caller on hold.	☐	☐
5. He's checking messages.	☐	☐
6. He's transcribing.	☐	☐

An Office   pages 126–129

Listen. Check (✓) the items that are in the supply closet.

OFFICE SUPPLIES INVENTORY

☐ clear tape   ☐ mailing labels

☐ correction fluid ☐ paper clips

☐ correction tape   ☐ rubber cement

☐ envelopes   ✓ staples

☐ glue   ☐ sticky notes

Computers   pages 130–131

Listen. Circle the words to complete the sentences.

1. Her <u>flash drive</u> / (<u>hard drive</u>) isn't working.

2. He is having problems with his <u>mouse / motherboard</u>.

3. She has a <u>desktop computer / laptop</u>.

4. The cable goes into the <u>printer / USB port</u>.

5. She probably needs a new <u>microprocessor / monitor</u>.

The Internet   pages 132–133

Listen. What is Carla doing? Check (✓) the answers.

1. ☐ **a.** addressing an email   ✓ **b.** typing a message
2. ☐ **a.** addressing an email   ☐ **b.** typing her password
3. ☐ **a.** clicking *Send*   ☐ **b.** clicking *Sign In*
4. ☐ **a.** checking her spelling   ☐ **b.** typing the subject
5. ☐ **a.** attaching a file   ☐ **b.** attaching a picture
6. ☐ **a.** typing her password   ☐ **b.** typing the subject

A Factory   pages 134–135

Look at page 134. Listen. Who's talking? Check (✓) the answers.

1. ✓ **a.** factory worker   ☐ **b.** shipping clerk
2. ☐ **a.** line supervisor   ☐ **b.** shipping clerk
3. ☐ **a.** designer   ☐ **b.** packer
4. ☐ **a.** factory owner   ☐ **b.** factory worker
5. ☐ **a.** line supervisor   ☐ **b.** packer
6. ☐ **a.** shipping clerk   ☐ **b.** order puller

Farming and Ranching pages 136–137

Listen. Where are they? Check (✓) the columns.

	Vegetable Garden	Field	Barn	Orchard	Vineyard	Corral
1.	✓					
2.						
3.						
4.						
5.						
6.						

Landscaping and Gardening pages 138–139

Listen. Check (✓) the jobs the gardening crew is doing today.

LAWNCARE
Landscaping and Gardening

- ✓ trim hedges
- ☐ plant trees
- ☐ mow lawn
- ☐ fertilize plants
- ☐ rake leaves
- ☐ water plants
- ☐ weed flower beds
- ☐ install sprinkler system

Trees and Plants pages 140–141

Look at page 140. Which trees or plants are they talking about?
Check (✓) the answers.

1. ☐ **a.** magnolia   ✓ **b.** redwood
2. ☐ **a.** holly   ☐ **b.** maple
3. ☐ **a.** dogwood   ☐ **b.** oak
4. ☐ **a.** oak   ☐ **b.** palm
5. ☐ **a.** birch   ☐ **b.** pine
6. ☐ **a.** pine   ☐ **b.** willow
7. ☐ **a.** cactus   ☐ **b.** poison ivy

Flowers pages 142–143

Listen. Complete the orders. Check (✓) the flowers.

1.

flo's flower Pot

Order Form
- ☐ carnations
- ☐ marigolds
- ☐ chrysanthemums
- ☐ roses
- ☐ irises
- ☑ tulips
- ☐ lilies
- ☐ violets

2. **flo's flower Pot**

Order Form
- ☐ carnations
- ☐ marigolds
- ☐ chrysanthemums
- ☐ roses
- ☐ irises
- ☐ tulips
- ☐ lilies
- ☐ violets

Construction pages 144–145

Listen. Check (✓) the supplies they are going to order.

R&J CONSTRUCTION SUPPLIES

- ☐ concrete
- ☑ tile
- ☐ bricks
- ☐ insulation
- ☐ stucco
- ☐ plywood
- ☐ lumber
- ☐ shingles

Tools and Building Supplies   pages 146–149

Look at pages 146–147. Listen. *True* or *False*? Check (✓) the answers.

	True	False
1.	✓	☐
2.	☐	☐
3.	☐	☐
4.	☐	☐
5.	☐	☐
6.	☐	☐

Household Problems and Repairs   pages 150–153

Listen. Write the number of the ad.

____ **a.** carpenter

____ **b.** electrician

____ **c.** exterminator

____ **d.** locksmith

____ **e.** plumber

_1_ **f.** repair person

____ **g.** roofer

Index

Index Key

Font

bold type = verbs or verb phrases (example: **catch**)

ordinary type = all other parts of speech (example: baseball)

ALL CAPS = unit titles (example: MATHEMATICS)

Initial caps = subunit titles (example: Equivalencies)

Symbols

✦ = word found in exercise band at bottom of page

Numbers/Letters

first number in **bold** type = page on which word appears

second number, or letter, following number in **bold** type = item number on page

(examples: cool [kōōl] **13**-5 means that the word *cool* is item number 5 on page 13;

across [ə krös/] **153**–G means that the word *across* is item G on page 153).

Pronunciation Guide

The index includes a pronunciation guide for all the words and phrases illustrated in the book. This guide uses symbols commonly found in dictionaries for native speakers. These symbols, unlike those used in pronunciation systems such as the International Phonetic Alphabet, tend to use English spelling patterns and so should help you to become more aware of the connections between written English and spoken English.

Consonants

[b] as in back [băk]	[k] as in key [kē]	[sh] as in shoe [shōō]
[ch] as in cheek [chēk]	[l] as in leaf [lēf]	[t] as in tape [tāp]
[d] as in date [dāt]	[m] as in match [măch]	[th] as in three [thrē]
[dh] as in this [dhĭs]	[n] as in neck [nĕk]	[v] as in vine [vīn]
[f] as in face [fās]	[ng] as in ring [rĭng]	[w] as in wait [wāt]
[g] as in gas [găs]	[p] as in park [pärk]	[y] as in yams [yămz]
[h] as in half [hăf]	[r] as in rice [rīs]	[z] as in zoo [zōō]
[j] as in jam [jăm]	[s] as in sand [sănd]	[zh] as in measure [mĕzhər]

Vowels

[ā] as in bake [bāk]	[ī] as in line [līn]	[ŏŏ] as in cook [kŏŏk]
[ă] as in back [băk]	[ĭ] as in lip [lĭp]	[ow] as in cow [kow]
[ä] as in car [kär] or box [bäks]	[ï] as in near [nïr]	[oy] as in boy [boy]
[ē] as in beat [bēt]	[ō] as in cold [kōld]	[ŭ] as in cut [kŭt]
[ĕ] as in bed [bĕd]	[ö] as in short [shört] or claw [klö]	[ü] as in curb [kürb]
[ë] as in bear [bër]	[ōō] as in cool [kōōl]	[ə] as in above [ə bŭv/]

All the pronunciation symbols used are alphabetical except for the schwa [ə]. The schwa is the most frequent vowel sound in English. If you use the schwa appropriately in unstressed syllables, your pronunciation will sound more natural.

Vowels before [r] are shown with the symbol [¨] to call attention to the special quality that vowels have before [r]. (Note that the symbols [ä] and [ö] are also used for vowels not followed by [r], as in *box* or *claw*.) You should listen carefully to native speakers to discover how these vowels actually sound.

Stress

This index follows the system for marking stress used in many dictionaries for native speakers.

1. Stress is not marked if a word consisting of a single syllable occurs by itself.

2. Where stress is marked, two levels are distinguished:

a bold accent [/] is placed after each syllable with primary (or strong) stress, a light accent [/] is placed after each syllable with secondary (or weaker) stress. In phrases and other combinations of words, stress is indicated for each word as it would be pronounced within the whole phrase.

Syllable Boundaries

Syllable boundaries are indicated by a single space or by a stress mark.

Note: The pronunciations shown in this index are based on patterns of American English. There has been no attempt to represent all of the varieties of American English. Students should listen to native speakers to hear how the language actually sounds in a particular region.

Index

Index

Index

Index